Annie Sloan's
DECORATIVE
STENCILLING
& STAMPING
A Step-by-Step Course

Annie Sloan's
DECORATIVE
STENCILLING
& STAMPING
A Step-by-Step Course

Photography by Geoff Dann

COLLINS & BROWN

First published in Great Britain in 1997
by Collins & Brown Limited
London House
Great Eastern Wharf
Parkgate Road
London SW11 4NQ

3 5 7 9 8 6 4 2

British Library Cataloguing-in-Publication Data:
A catalogue record for this book
is available from the British Library.

ISBN 1 85585 2497 (hardback edition)

ISBN 1 85585 4244 (paperback edition)

Conceived, edited and designed by
Collins & Brown Limited

Editor Colin Ziegler
Assistant Editor Claire Waite
Art Director Roger Bristow
Designer Steve Wooster
DTP Designer Claire Graham
Photographer Geoff Dann

Reproduction by Daylight Colour Art, Singapore

Printed and bound in Portugal

Contents

Introduction

STENCILING AND STAMPING provide customized ways to apply patterns to walls, furniture, and fabrics. You can choose among a wide range of patterns and a virtually unlimited variety of styles. Both of these techniques have been in use since ancient times in many different cultures, often originally for fabric decoration. For example, early people of the Fijian islands cut stencils from the tough leaves of the banana. The Japanese often created stencils from the bark of the mulberry tree. Stamping has its roots in a broad range of traditions, which provide rich inspiration for modern stamping. Ancient Mexican stamps were made from clay. In both Africa and Indonesia, stamps were and are still carved from wood.

Using Stencil Brushes

ABOVE This most traditional type of stenciling (see pp. 38–43) can be used for all styles of design, from formal Victorian designs to folk art, depending on the method and colors that you choose. You apply a small amount of paint with a short-bristled stencil brush, either by stippling, wiping, or swirling on the paint. This tray was done with the wiped brush technique to give the apples a three-dimensional look.

Using Rollers

ABOVE This quick technique (see pp. 44–47) works especially well on walls and for large, open areas of stenciling. You coat a sponge roller with paint, wipe off the excess, then roll the paint over the stencil. The results vary from solid to lightly textured, depending on how hard, and how many times, you roll the paint on. This wall design – a pattern inspired by Chinese wallpaper – was rolled in blue over white.

Modern stenciling draws on many of the different periods and countries from which this method of pattern-making developed. From the delicate, intricate work of Japanese stencils to the bold, but complex, African designs, from the naive simplicity of Pennsylvania Dutch, Dutch, and Scandinavian folk art to the classical formality of Victorian designs, you can draw inspiration, combine, or adapt to make innovative stencils of your own.

Stenciling, the first part of this book (see pp. 18–63), explores and explains the technique from a variety of starting places. Beginning with the use of ready-designed stencils for the novice (see pp. 22–25), you can move on to techniques for tackling stenciling intricacies, such as repeats and corners (see pp. 30–37). Once you have mastered these, consider the many ways of making patterns and converting designs into stencils, stamps, and rollers. You can choose any of several ways to apply paint, using brushes, rollers, and sprays (see pp. 38–53), and experiment with these methods to create different decorative effects. Hand painting – a development of

Reverse Stenciling

ABOVE Stencils make patterns by blocking out some parts of a design. In reverse stenciling (see pp. 58–63), the part that you normally discard remains, and you apply paint around it to form a silhouette. You can use the central part of traditional stencils, stickers in various forms, and natural shapes such as leaves. On this lamp base, circular stickers were put to good use.

Using Spray Paints

ABOVE For fine, delicate, and intricate designs like this one, the spray technique (see pp. 48–53) is the best choice. It results in a very even, finely dotted application of color. You can merge the dots for more solid coverage by using a greater amount of spray. Any of the spray paints sold for use by artists and model-makers, or for vehicle spraying work well.

Hand Painting with Stencils

ABOVE To create the effect shown on this panel (see pp. 54–57), which echoes hand-painted Chinese wallpaper, you begin with a stencil, applied with a brush, roller, or spray. You then paint simple lines, spots, and other designs on top and around the design, using a fine artist's brush.

stenciling in which you use the stencil as a background and add hand painting – and reverse stenciling – in which you use the part of the original stencil you usually discard as a silhouette – provide opportunities for further customizing your choice of design (see pp. 54–63).

Stamping, the second part of the book, deals with ways to create and use decorative stamps (see pp. 64–87). You can use objects found around the house, make your own stamps, and use decorator's rollers. Found objects – household items such as corks, bubble wrap, paper cups, nails, corrugated paper, and numerous other ordinary items (see pp. 72–75) – provide the building blocks for pattern making in a simple but exciting way. As an alternative, you can use Styrofoam/polystyrene, sponges, and potatoes to make stamps with interesting textures and create unique patterns on walls and furniture (see pp. 76–81). Rollers (see pp. 82–87) have long been used, particularly for wallpaper and fabric designs, to make simple stripes and checks. Ready-cut patterned rollers, or foam rollers into which you can carve your own pattern, add a lively dimension to a simple technique.

Using Found Objects

ABOVE *For this technique (see pp. 72–75) you apply paint to readily available items, such as corks, nail heads, paper cups, and lids, then stamp them onto a surface to create patterns. This simple, direct method permits you great freedom of expression, allowing as many styles and designs as you have the imagination to create. The Australian Aboriginal design on this tabletop was made using nail heads dipped in different-colored paints.*

Making Stamps

ABOVE *From the humble potato print to more intricate stamps made from Styrofoam/polystyrene or sponge (see pp. 76–81), stamps or "blocks" provide a wonderful means to make patterns reminiscent of old block-printed designs. This African frog design was cut out of Styrofoam/polystyrene and stamped in rows.*

You can use the same stencil or stamp design in many different ways, giving it different treatments and colors to create different results. The last pages of the book (see pp. 88–91) show you how to combine techniques to create stunning and unusual stenciled and stamped effects, giving designs on walls and furniture added depth and interest.

Decorative Stenciling and Stamping offers as much about applying stencils and stamps in various ways as it does about creating them. Throughout the book you will find step-by-step instructions, variations and color combinations to try, potential pitfalls to avoid, and countless ideas showing how to use the techniques on walls and large and small pieces of furniture. Learning to use backgrounds effectively will give depth and character to your work, as will a knowledgeable choice of paints, varnishes, waxes, and finishes (see pp. 12–17).

By approaching all the techniques covered in this book with a spirit of adventure and experimentation, you will find you can transform something commonplace into something unique.

Making Cylinder Stamps with Rollers
LEFT Rollers offer not only a superb way of making stripes and tartan effects, but also a quick, controllable way of creating repeating patterns (see pp. 82–87). Here, a ready-made rubber roller with a three-dimensional pattern was used, but you could just as easily cut a pattern yourself out of a sponge roller.

Preparing Surfaces

TOOLS & MATERIALS

Paint stripper

Screw-driver

Protective rubber gloves

Strong bristle brush for applying paint stripper

Coarse steelwool

Sponge

Scraper

Medium-grade sandpaper and wooden block

Proprietary filler

Water-base paint and brush for applying it

YOU CAN MAKE SURE that your stenciling and stamping projects will last a long time by first preparing the surface well. If you apply your design to old varnish or paint, the work is likely to peel, crack, or chip. First, try rubbing off any old varnish with sandpaper. If it comes off easily there is no need to use paint stripper. Old paint and more stubborn varnish will probably need to be stripped. Varnish generally comes off readily, but several layers of paint will prove more difficult. Once the surface is clean, you will need to fill and rub down any holes and cracks.

Using Paint Stripper

1 Remove any handles, unless they are made of wood. Test carved parts of furniture to see if they are wood, by applying paint stripper to a small area. Plaster and some plastics will dissolve in paint stripper.

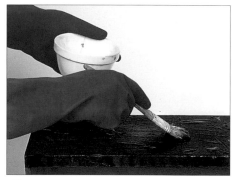

2 Paint stripper is highly caustic and burns the skin, so use protective gloves and protect the surrounding area. Apply the stripper with a strong bristle brush and leave on until the old coat has bubbled up.

3 Remove the softened varnish or paint right away, using coarse steelwool and working in the direction of the wood's grain. Do not allow the stripper to dry or you will have difficulty removing it.

4 Wipe off paint or varnish particles with a damp cloth or sponge – if you plan to use oil-base varnish later use turpentine instead of water. Reapply stripper and rub down again if necessary.

Getting a Smooth Surface

1 With some items of furniture, such as this chest of drawers (right), you can avoid using paint stripper and remove unwanted coverings with a scraper.

2 To remove the last remnants of paint or varnish, rub the surface with medium-grade sandpaper wrapped around a wooden block (the block keeps the surface flat).

3 This action may reveal holes and cracks in the surface. Use a scraper to fill these with ready-made filler. Put a thin layer on and allow to dry for about 20 minutes.

4 Cover the surface with water-base paint and allow to dry. A flat coat of paint reveals any surface unevenness and indicates areas still needing to be filled.

5 Fill any further cracks and holes and allow to dry. Rub down well with a piece of medium-grade sandpaper around a wooden block. Paint and rub down again if necessary.

PREPARING WALLS

Unless you want to achieve a distressed stenciled effect, walls need to be smooth and in good condition. Roller stenciling requires a particularly smooth surface. Spray stenciling also needs a flat surface, so that the stencil adheres properly to the wall and the spray does not seep under the stencil and leave a blurred pattern. Stamping and roller techniques usually require a smooth surface to obtain a good print, but experiment on your surface before filling it – a slightly uneven surface can create an appealing effect.

• Any flaky paintwork needs to be repaired by rubbing down the wall with coarse sandpaper and repainting it.

• If you are going to stamp or do detailed, delicate stenciling and the wall is pitted or cracked, fill the holes with a ready-made filler, as described in Step 3 of *Getting a Smooth Surface* (left).

• You can work on painted wallpaper or lining paper, as long as it is properly adhered. You may be able to use the brush stenciling technique on some textured wallpaper, but other techniques may blotch, so that you cannot see the pattern properly.

• You can brush-stencil on old walls, where the surface is uneven and slightly rough, to give a country-style effect.

Choosing Backgrounds

THE TYPE OF BACKGROUND you choose will depend on the type of stenciling or stamping you plan to do. A plain, one-color background works well with an uneven sprayed stencil. A textured background enhances a solid brush stencil or stamp. A crackleglaze texture in strong colors looks best with a simple roller stencil. The rule of thumb: the busier the background texture, the plainer the stenciling method you should use.

Mixed Color

1 Take two similar shades of paint, such as a darker and lighter tone of the same color. Paint an irregular shape with the first color.

2 Using the same brush, while the first color is still wet, paint on the second color to finish covering the desired surface.

The result should be irregular, cloudy areas of paint that change subtly from light to medium tones.

Dry Brush

With a dry brush, pick up a little paint in a color that is close in tone to the dry painted base. Paint in straight lines across the surface, using just the tip of the brush.

This technique releases a little paint and leaves a slightly striped effect.

Frottage

1 Coat a dry painted base with diluted paint (1 part water to 2 parts paint) in a color close in tone.

2 Place a piece of newspaper on top. Flatten it out with your hands to absorb the paint.

3 Remove the paper immediately to reveal an unevenly textured background of small lines, created by the grain of the newspaper.

By doing this technique quickly, in sections of one newspaper size area, you will create a unified pattern.

Crackleglaze

1 Apply a coat of crackleglaze medium over a dry coat of water-base paint. Crackleglaze is a transparent medium that darkens the basecoat slightly. Leave to dry thoroughly for approximately 20 minutes.

2 Apply an even, not too thick, coat of water-base paint on top of the medium. Within 5 minutes cracks should appear.

When the crackle effect is completely dry – in about 30 minutes – apply your stencil or stamp design.

Paints

ALTHOUGH SPECIFIC PAINTS are made for stenciling and stamping, you can in fact use any paint. The particular paint you choose depends on your own preferences, and the type of tools you use to paint your stencil. Generally you should avoid paints that are too diluted since they may seep under the stencil; but if you want to use a roller, you will need a paint that is sufficiently liquid, yet opaque, so that you can roll the roller through it. An intricate stencil may work best with spray paint, while for specialized projects oil-base or watercolor paints, waxes or special fabric paints may be desirable. The trick with any paint, however, is to use it sparingly. A small amount goes a long way.

Water-base Paints

ABOVE AND RIGHT Water-base paints, also known as acrylic paints, dry quickly, allowing you to add to both the stencil and the surface without fear of smudging. You can also wash the tools in water after use. Artist's acrylic paint is solid and best used only for brush stenciling. Decorator's paint is made especially for stenciling and stamping. Household paint, such as vinyl or latex/ emulsion, tends to be too liquid to use.

Decorator's paint

Artist's acrylic paint

Artist's oil paint

Oil-base paint

Oil-base Paints

ABOVE Oil-base paints – especially artist's paints, which come in many colors – work well for stenciling. But they dry slowly, so overlapping stencil designs may cause some smudging. Oil-base paints are not recommended for stamping.

Spray paint

Spray Paints

ABOVE AND RIGHT Spray paints are useful for stenciling on various surfaces, including glass and fabric. You can even use spray paints intended for cars. Breathing the fumes of spray paints is hazardous, so wear a face mask and work in a well ventilated area.

Metallic Waxes

Gold-colored metallic wax

ABOVE AND RIGHT Metallic waxes are useful for brush stenciling. They are particularly helpful to beginners because the wax is dry and therefore does not run or smudge.

Metallic wax stick

Fabric paints

Fabric Paints

ABOVE Fabric paints are effective and washable for both stenciling and stamping. You can use ordinary paints instead, but the color will wash out, leaving only a faint pattern.

Artist's watercolor paint

Watercolor Paints

ABOVE Watercolor paints cannot be used for stamping or stenciling, because they are too thin. But they are ideal for hand painting over a solid stenciled base (see pp. 54–57).

Varnishes and Waxes

Varnishes and waxes provide protection and finish. Gloss – which creates the shiniest finish – and satin varnish (both oil- and water-base) offer most protection. Oil-base varnish gives a slightly yellowed appearance that adds extra depth and richness. Flat varnishes do not hold up as well and can absorb oil marks, causing dark stains.

Waxes also protect your work, though not as well as varnishes. They produce a softer, mellower finish, which you can buff to a silky sheen.

Using Varnish

Apply varnish in a thin, even layer using a soft, flat-ended brush. Here, oil-base varnish was applied to finish a water-base crack-leglaze (a water-base varnish would be affected by the crackle medium). Choose a varnish according to the final effect you prefer.

One coat of varnish should be sufficient to protect the stencil, but two coats, as used here, will hold up longer.

Using Wax

Apply a liberal amount of dark toluene-free wax (toluene acts as a paint remover), using very soft steelwool, and rub in well (inset). Leave for about 5 minutes, then wipe off with a soft rag (right), buffing the surface to achieve a sheen.

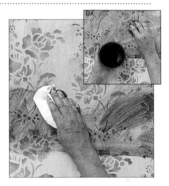

The wax darkens the surface of the stencil and protects it. Use a darker wax, or leave the wax on longer, for a richer effect. Use a clear wax for a lighter effect.

Coloring Varnish

1 You can add pigment to either water- or oil-base varnish. Here, a water-base varnish was used. Coat the surface with the varnish, then work it in well using a soft, flat-ended brush.

2 While the varnish is still wet either dab your brush in the powder pigment, or sprinkle pigment directly onto the surface and blend it in to obtain the desired effect. Test pigments before use, as they vary considerably.

In this case the finished effect is a blue tinge. Brown pigments create an antiqued effect, while a mixture of several pigments produces a more mottled effect.

Using Crackle Varnish

1 To get a crackled effect add a coat of water-base varnish over a nearly dry coat of oil-base varnish and warm the surface slightly, using a hair drier if necessary, to make the varnish crack. When the surface is completely dry emphasize the cracks by filling them in with dark artist's oil paint.

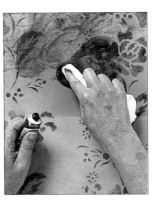

2 To protect the surface and prevent it from cracking further, cover it with a final coat of oil-base varnish.

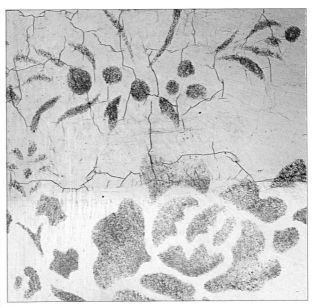

This varnish gives an antiqued effect and looks best on a traditional stencil done in muted colors.

Stenciling

Tools and Materials

ALL THE STENCILING techniques call for three main types of equipment: materials to design and cut stencils (below); materials for attaching and marking out stencils (right); and materials for printing stencil designs (below right). Concentrate first on learning how to apply paint using brushes – to start, a medium-size brush is probably best – a small roller, and some sponges to experiment with.

Designing and Cutting Stencils

BELOW AND RIGHT *Stencils are cut from poster board, also known as stencil card, or acetate using a craft knife or heat knife. When using a craft knife, cut on a cutting board that leaves no score marks that might interfere with subsequent cutting. When using a heat knife (see p. 24) – the quickest and easiest tool for cutting acetate stencils – cut on a piece of glass.*

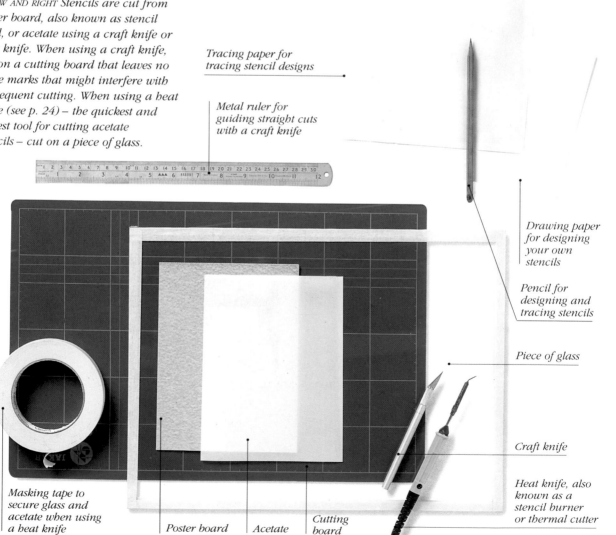

Tracing paper for tracing stencil designs

Metal ruler for guiding straight cuts with a craft knife

Drawing paper for designing your own stencils

Pencil for designing and tracing stencils

Piece of glass

Craft knife

Heat knife, also known as a stencil burner or thermal cutter

Masking tape to secure glass and acetate when using a heat knife

Poster board

Acetate

Cutting board

Positioning and Attaching Stencils

BELOW AND RIGHT To make sure your design is aligned, mark out your stencil positions, especially on large surfaces, before applying paint. You can make a simple chalk line on a wall by wiping a piece of string with children's chalk, but the chalk line shown here is more efficient. Create a simple plumb line with string and mounting putty/ Blu-Tack. Use masking tape (see p. 20) or repositioning glue/Spray Mount to attach the stencil to the surface and newspaper to mask areas you don't want stenciled. The fumes of the spray can be hazardous, so wear a face mask and work in a well-ventilated area.

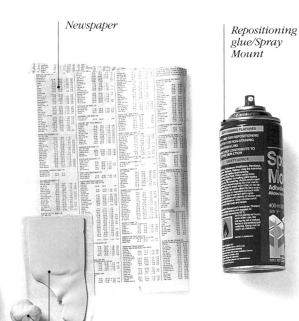

Newspaper

Repositioning glue/Spray Mount

String

Chalk line

Mounting putty/Blu-Tack

Applying Paint

BELOW AND RIGHT Apply paint to your stencils using brushes, rollers, and sponges. Large rollers are best for painting wall stencils, especially if you are using only one color. For brush stenciling you can start off with only one or two brushes, but you may need more as your stencils become more intricate and colorful.

Large roller for use on walls and large stencil designs

Sponge as alternative to brushes

Roller tray for use as a palette

Soft-bristled stencil brushes

Stencil brush with two bristled ends for applying two colors easily on one design

Large, stiff-bristled stencil brushes for applying paint to large stencil designs

Small roller for use on furniture or small stencil designs

Cutting Ready-designed Stencils

Stencil Examples

A poster board stencil is heavier than an acetate stencil but is more rigid, making it easier to handle and so more suitable for large designs. An acetate stencil can be more difficult to handle but is easier to cut and suitable for small, intricate designs.

YOU CAN BUY READY-DESIGNED stencils from art supply and decorating stores. Some of these are precut. Others come on poster board or acetate and need to be cut out. Still others consist of a design you need to transfer to poster board or acetate and then cut out. Both poster board and acetate can be cut with a strong, sharp, craft knife. While poster board is inexpensive, many people find that cutting it with a craft knife is hard work. For an easier and quicker method that does not rely so much on hand pressure, you may want to stick to acetate. Keep in mind that acetate is more difficult to handle than poster board, particularly when producing very large designs, because it can bend and curls easily.

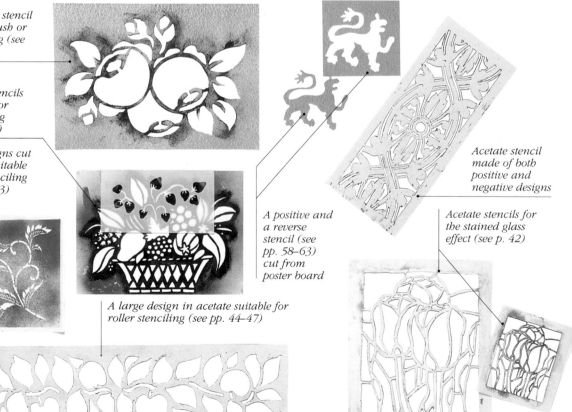

A poster board stencil suitable for brush or roller stenciling (see pp. 38–47)

Two acetate stencils most suitable for brush stenciling (see pp. 38–43)

Delicate designs cut in acetate, suitable for spray stenciling (see pp. 48–53)

A positive and a reverse stencil (see pp. 58–63) cut from poster board

Acetate stencil made of both positive and negative designs

Acetate stencils for the stained glass effect (see p. 42)

A large design in acetate suitable for roller stenciling (see pp. 44–47)

Cutting a Poster Board Stencil

1 *Preprinted stencils from books are normally printed on poster board. To make the poster board paint-proof, dab the entire surface with a mixture of 1 part boiled lin-seed oil to 1 part turpentine. Leave to dry for 10 minutes.*

2 *Cut out the design, using a sharp craft knife. Hold the knife like a pencil and cut on a hard-surfaced cutting board such as the one shown. Cutting on wood or poster board may cause score lines that affect the stencil cutting.*

3 *To cut a curve, turn the poster board while keeping the craft knife in one place (right). This helps create a line that is smooth, rather than jagged or angular.*

Tracing a Stencil

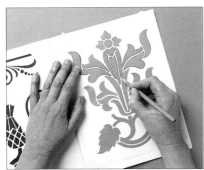

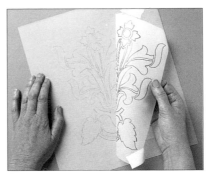

1 *Fix a piece of tracing paper or waxed paper (which is less trans-parent) over the design with masking tape, and trace the design with a soft pencil (2B is ideal).*

2 *Turn the tracing paper over and tape it to a sheet of paint-proof poster board, leaving a border of 1–2in/2.5–5cm around the design. Trace over your pencil lines.*

3 *Check the imprint left by your pencil before removing the tracing paper. The poster board is now ready for cutting, as shown above.*

Cutting Acetate with a Heat Knife

WARNING

Heat knives, also known as stencil burners and thermal cutters, are available in the better-equipped art supply stores. They become extremely hot, so should always be handled with great care. Make sure you follow the instructions on the packaging.

1 Place your stencil design on a table. Secure a sheet of glass over the design with masking tape. Tape a sheet of acetate on top of the glass, with your design in a central position.

2 Plug in the heat knife and allow it to warm up for a few minutes. Check by testing it on a spare piece of acetate. Place the point of the knife along a line of the design and start moving it slowly across the acetate.

PITFALLS

If you move the heat knife too quickly, it may skid across the surface, missing part of the stencil design (below). If you leave the heat knife on the acetate for too long, you may make an unwanted, over-large hole (bottom). Concentrate on moving the knife at a steady pace.

3 After completing the design, remove the sheet of acetate (right). Some of the shapes will fall out, but others may stick to the glass. You may need to carefully push some shapes out with your fingers to remove them completely.

RIGHT Heat knife moved too quickly

LEFT Heat knife left on too long

Adjusting a Design

1 By tracing your design onto acetate before cutting it out, you can adjust an unsuitable design, adding bridges (see p. 29) to avoid too many long, unbroken shapes. Use a special crayon, called a china marker or grease pencil, available from art supply stores, to draw on acetate.

2 If you make a mistake in the design, you can rub it away with a little turpentine on the end of a cotton swab.

3 Cut out the shapes, taking care not to cut the bridges – here, the gaps between leaf shapes and stem.

Punching Holes

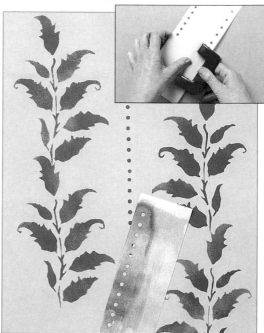

It is difficult to cut out perfectly round holes; they often become rather angular. You can quickly make unbroken holes using a hole punch (inset). Here, a row of holes has been cut to make a long line on a wall design (above).

Repairing a Stencil

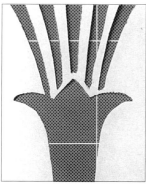

Sometimes you make a cut where there should not be one, leave out a bridge (as here), or break a stencil while using it.

1 You can do a quick repair with good-quality adhesive tape. Stick tape first on one side of the broken area, then on the other side, to make a double layer of tape over the break.

2 Cut out any unwanted parts of tape using a sharp craft knife (above). The remaining tape now forms the lost bridge (right), and the stencil is ready for use.

Designing Stencils

Stencil Sources

Look for stencil designs in a variety of places. Here fabrics, tiles, china plates, and books of designs have been used. You can photocopy and enlarge these to the required size before adapting them to produce your own design.

ONCE YOU HAVE experimented with ready-made stencils, you may want to design your own stencil for a particular project. First decide on the subject and style of the stencil. You may want to adapt a design from curtain fabric or a decorative item in the same room as your project. There are also many books containing black-and-white designs that you can adapt. The photocopier makes it easy for you to enlarge designs to exactly the required size. Bridges, or ties, are the essential pieces on the stencil that connect the separate parts (see *Adding Bridges* p. 29); they can also serve as a decorative device, if used cleverly, to break up large blocks of color and help to give a design depth and definition.

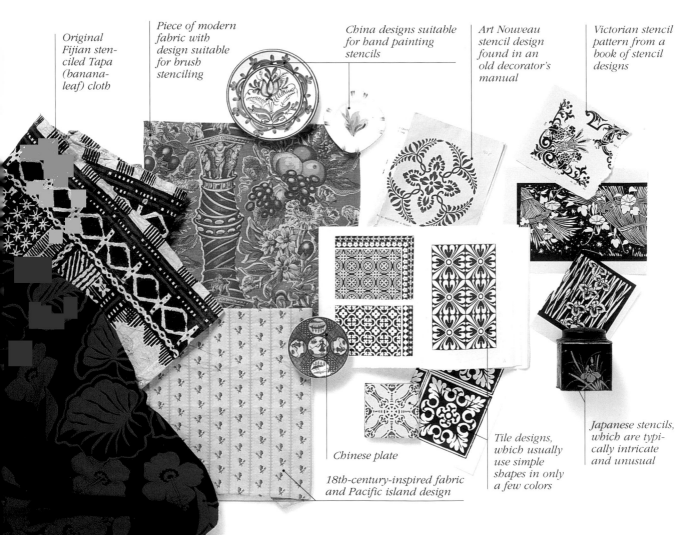

Original Fijian stenciled Tapa (banana-leaf) cloth

Piece of modern fabric with design suitable for brush stenciling

China designs suitable for hand painting stencils

Art Nouveau stencil design found in an old decorator's manual

Victorian stencil pattern from a book of stencil designs

Chinese plate

18th-century-inspired fabric and Pacific island design

Tile designs, which usually use simple shapes in only a few colors

Japanese stencils, which are typically intricate and unusual

Adapting a Design

Wherever you find your design – there are many books of copyright-free designs taken from wallpaper, fabrics, china, tiles, and carpets – turning it into a stencil requires adaptation. Some designs are very simple to adapt; others need more ingenuity.

1 Choose a tile (or other) design from a source book and enlarge it on a photocopier to the required size.

2 Block out areas not needed (such as the ribbon here), with a felt-tip pen, marking these in as bridges.

3 Using a white correction pen, block out any unnecessary details (for example, the dog's paws) that are likely to become filled with paint.

4 Trace the design onto poster board and cut it out (see p. 23). You can still adapt the design at this stage. Here, a long tongue (see Adding Bridges p. 29) is being eliminated.

The Finished Stencil and Print

RIGHT The original design has been made into a stencil by simplifying the design and adding bridges that support the stencil and break up large blocks of color.

POSITIVE/NEGATIVE

A stencil design consists of positive and/or negative shapes. A negative shape occurs when you cut the actual motif out of the poster board. A positive shape occurs when you cut out the areas surrounding the motif. More complex designs use both shapes.

ABOVE Inside the circle the motif is a positive shape. The small clover leaf motif that has been cut into this makes a negative shape.

A positive stencil and print

A negative stencil and print

ABOVE The same design was reversed to make both a positive and negative shape. The positive shape needs a border round it to hold the design in the center.

Making a Simple Stencil

Making your own stencil can be easy, if you use simple shapes and designs. For example, you could make the flower shape below into a stencil in numerous ways, with little change to the basic idea. You simply alter some parts of the design to make bridges, so that the shapes stay together.

1 *Select a design from a book of patterns. Then enlarge it on a photocopier until the pattern is the size you want.*

2 *This design would be most suitable for making a stamp (see p. 69); once you remove the central circle and rings, nothing holds the design together. To make a stencil from this, you need to add bridges.*

3 *There are many ways to make a stencil from this particular design. Here are four interpretations, each emphasizing a different aspect of the same basic shape.*

The outer ring has been reduced to small dots (machinery cog effect).

The outer circle has been made into wedges (wheel effect).

The "petals" have become positive shapes (stained glass window effect).

Two stencils have been used to emphasize the central spot (sun effect), the more intricate stencil first, then the simple circle.

Adding Bridges

Long tongues in a design (right) tend to lift up or catch as you try to apply the paint. Any very thin, negative shape clogs up easily, while a thin, positive shape is in danger of breaking. To avoid these pitfalls you should leave bridges in your stencil, solid strips inserted into the design to join tongues to the other parts of the stencil, keeping all parts firmly attached (far right).

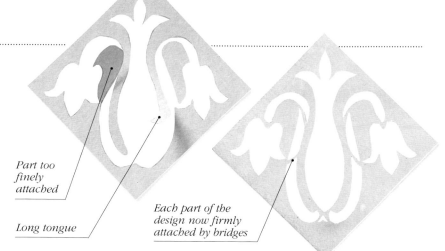

Part too finely attached

Long tongue

Each part of the design now firmly attached by bridges

Symmetrical Stencils

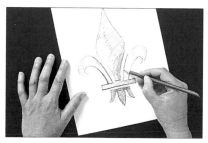

1 *It is very difficult to make a design look completely symmetrical. For some designs, such as a fleur-de-lis, symmetry is important. Begin by drawing your stencil design.*

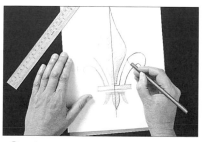

2 *Place tracing paper over your design and draw a line down the middle of it. Trace whichever half of the design you prefer, using a soft pencil and making a good, solid line.*

3 *Reverse the tracing paper, then place it centrally on a piece of paint-proof poster board (see p. 23). Retrace your pencil lines, so that they transfer to the poster board.*

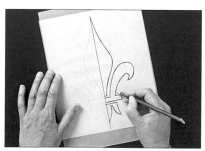

4 *Turn the tracing paper over again, then line up the perpendicular pencil line against the other half of the design. Trace over the shape to make the completely symmetrical design (right). You can use the same method on acetate.*

Repeat and Random Stencils

Repeating Houses

This motif was applied in a regular design, but the color has been varied. Although there is a wide range of colors, the tones are quite similar, preventing one color from dominating.

STENCILING ALLOWS you to decorate a wall or piece of furniture with a unique pattern. Even if the stencil motif itself is not unique, you can use the motif in unique ways. The traditional stencil creates a repeating pattern, of which there are numerous variations, as the following pages show. The execution of the design needs careful attention and measuring, but it results in your own hand-painted wallpaper or fabric. A less common use of the stencil motif calls for a more random unmeasured application. Practice on a piece of scrap paper first in order to work out your design.

Random Landscape

LEFT Six stencils were combined in a random pattern to make this landscape, using an assortment of colors.

Regular Repeat

BELOW These two tile-like stencils were used to create a repeat pattern. Many variations exist on this basic theme, such as reversing the stencil every second row.

Overprinted Stencil

RIGHT This red, lightly striped checkerboard stencil was printed in a regular pattern, providing a controlled background for the randomly stenciled oak leaves.

Simple Repeats

1 Print one motif. Move the stencil to one side. Mark the edge of the first motif on the acetate with a china marker (see p. 25).

2 Print the design again. Do not paint over the china marker mark, as this shows you where to place the stencil each time.

3 For the next row, place the stencil in position halfway between the motifs in the row above.

4 As before, mark the edge of the previous motifs on the acetate to act as a guideline.

5 The stencil is printed in a brick pattern, with the motifs in the second row positioned halfway between the motifs in the row above. Each motif in this particular pattern is printed facing in the same direction.

Using Two Stencils

1 Print the first stencil. Position a second, identical stencil in reverse. Mark the first motif as in Simple Repeats (above) and print.

2 Place the dry first stencil upside-down and below the first motif. Mark on the acetate as in Simple Repeats and print.

3 Place the second stencil upside-down, below the second motif. Mark the position of the motifs above and to the side before printing.

4 By repeating Steps 1–3 across the whole surface you get a pattern of twisting wreaths or cascades of flowers, with an abstract pattern of leaves.

Repeat Patterns

A single stencil can form the basis of many different repeat patterns. Try turning it upside down, flipping it over, or printing it in stripes. Imagine that your stencil is on a single tile, and arrange it in a simple checkerboard pattern, or create a half drop pattern, in which the motifs in the second row are printed halfway between those above, instead of directly underneath.

Circular pattern made by turning the design three times

Stencil reversed and used in a half drop

Same direction but different colors

Stripes made by reversing the stencil

Spacing out a Repeat Pattern

Executing a repeat pattern on a wall where the motifs are some distance apart requires careful measuring and the use of a plumb line (see p. 21). Start the design in the center of the main wall and work outward to the corners. This becomes particularly important with large designs, if you want to maximize the effect. Alternatively, measure the wall and divide it into equal sections, then fit your stencil into each section. This will eliminate half-stencil shapes on the wall.

1 *Attach some scrap paper or newspaper to the wall or surface that you are going to decorate. Practice stenciling your repeat pattern on this paper to test how it will look, how the pattern will repeat, and what its measurements are.*

2 *To adjust the design, print the motif on paper and try it in different positions. Here, the design was printed upside down to give variation.*

3 *Measure the distance between the trial motifs, from left to right and from top to bottom. Make a note of this, so that you can use the same distances on the actual wall.*

4 *Start the design in the middle of the wall. Make a plumb line using mounting putty/Blu-Tack on the bottom of a length of string, and attach it to the wall with mounting putty/Blu-Tack. Line up the center of the stencil motif with the string.*

5 *Move the string aside and stencil the pattern onto the wall. Roller stenciling is the quickest method for decorating walls, but you should use the method you feel most comfortable with.*

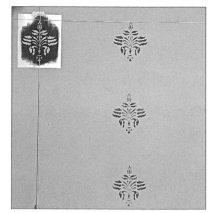

6 Using the measurements from your trial motifs and the plumb line, position and print the stencil below the first motif. Continue to the bottom of your surface.

7 Measure to one side and reposition the plumb line. Using more string and mounting putty/Blu-Tack, make a horizontal line to mark the position of the top of the motifs.

8 Place the stencil in position with the plumb line in the middle of the design and the top of the design lined up with the horizontal string, then print it.

9 Repeat Steps 4–8, making vertical lines, until your surface is covered.

10 Now place the upside down stencil in between the printed motifs. Use the plumb line to position the stencil.

11 Print the design and fill in all the gaps, working in vertical lines, as before (inset). The finished work should have a regular, overall pattern (above). But by using the stencil upside down every second line you create a slight undulating effect, which is not at first apparent.

Stenciling a Corner: The Gap Method

When stenciling a whole wall with a large design, you need a plan for coping with the corners. A large, intricate, acetate stencil might well fall apart, or become floppy and uncontrollable when used there. This method of leaving a small gap in the corner offers a neat solution. The size of the gap you leave is up to you, but if it is larger than ½in/1.25cm the effect may appear disjointed.

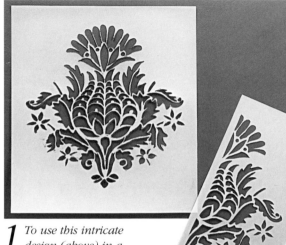

1 To use this intricate design (above) in a corner, cut out just half of it, leaving a strip of acetate along the middle edge (right).

2 Place the half-stencil in position in the corner and print the design. Use a piece of paper, stuck down with repositioning glue/Spray Mount, on the adjacent wall to protect it, especially when the acetate strip is narrow.

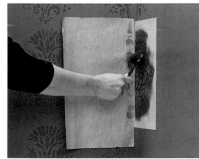

3 When the corner stencil is dry, move on to the adjacent wall. Place the half-stencil in the correct position, measuring it if necessary. Print the design as before.

4 Continue stenciling along the length of the wall. The final result (right) shows the neat corner effect that this gap method creates.

Stenciling a Corner: The Cut Method

If the design is small and has little detail, it may be possible to cut the stencil at any point without the design falling apart. This border design consists of one whole design, plus a repeat of part of the pattern. This enables you to place the design over the already executed stencil so that the pattern repeats in the correct way. You may find it easier to use several stencils for one room.

1 Place the stencil on the wall, over-lapping the repeated part of the design with the stenciling already done. Print the design on the wall.

2 At the corner, mark in pencil where the stencil needs to be cut. It may be possible to print a tightly folded acetate stencil, but keeping it in position is very difficult.

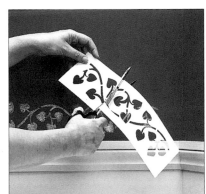

3 Cut the stencil along the pencil mark. If you have only one sten-cil, you should leave the corners until last, marking their positions on the acetate as you go along.

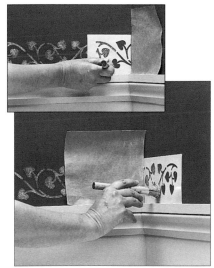

4 Print the design, placing some scrap paper on the adjacent wall (inset) to protect it from paint. When the paint is dry, do the same in reverse on the adjacent wall (above), continuing the pattern.

5 The finished effect gives a continuous pattern, which is particularly important for the scroll design of this stenciled border. The technique used here is brush stippling, which gives a soft, light effect.

Using Stencil Brushes

Brush-stenciled Table
This simple table has been given a country treatment. Old-fashioned, muted colors were applied over its original worn brown basecoat, using the stippled, swirled, and wiped techniques (see p. 39) to highlight the texture of the fruit and foliage.

Brushes work especially well for creating both traditional country designs, which use a painterly style, and formal Victorian designs, in which each part of the design is done in a different color. You can use the brush to stipple – lightly dab the surface with the tip of the brush – to create a dotted effect, swirl it in all directions for a soft effect, or wipe from side to side to create a striped effect. By wiping the brush from the tip to the base of a leaf shape, you can use the brushstroke to define the leaf. Carrying small amounts of color from one part of a design to another will add unity to your design. For example, if you are using green on a leaf, add a little green to the edges of the flower, and vice versa. As with all forms of stenciling, the trick is to use very little, dry paint (see p. 14).

TOOLS & MATERIALS

Roller tray
used as a
palette

Medium-size
stencil brushes

Sponge, an
alternative
to brushes

Acetate stencils

Paper towel
for removing
excess paint

Masking tape

Repositioning
glue/Spray Mount

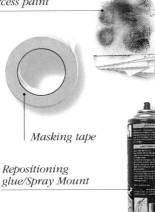

The Basic Technique

1 To get a striped effect on
this leaf (above), pull
the brush from tip to stem
in a wiping motion (right).

2 To create a softer effect
than the stripes creat-
ed by the wiped technique,
swirl the brush around in
several directions, as on
the pumpkin.

3 When combining several colors, as on the
pear (inset), use the brush to stipple, lightly
pushing the bristles vertically onto the surface to
create small dots of color.

4 You can also combine
the three different
techniques – wiping,
swirling, and stippling –
on parts of the design. To
give the design coherence,
one color should overlap
onto several areas.

Using Metallic Wax

You can use metallic wax (see p. 15) to imitate bronze powder work (see p. 55). After stenciling, allow the wax to dry overnight, then protect it with a coat of shellac followed by a coat of oil-base varnish (see pp. 16–17). For the best effect use wax against a dark, rich background or on off-white.

1 Dip the brush into some metallic wax. Wipe the excess on a paper towel. Apply the wax in a swirling motion (above and right).

2 To give a three-dimensional feel, add more metallic wax in a different shade. Here, a dark and a light gold metallic wax were used together.

Brush Stenciling on Fabric

Special paints are available for use on fabric (see p. 15). These usually need to be ironed afterward, to set the paint, making it wash resistant. If the fabric will not need washing, you can use ordinary water-base paint instead. Washing will not completely remove this paint, but will leave a soft effect.

1 Put absorbent paper under the fabric – the paint will seep through – and tape down the fabric to keep it flat. Fix the stencil in place. Apply a small amount of paint in a swirling motion.

2 Apply a second color in selected places with the same technique. This will give the design a three-dimensional quality. Be careful not to apply too much paint, as a little goes a long way.

3 Before you move on to another part of the surface, check to see how the fabric is receiving the paint. Some fabrics are more absorbent than others.

4 Here, the design was carried through in a half-drop repeat (see pp. 32–33). The slight variation in color each time the stencil is applied is all part of the hand-painted look.

Using a Sponge

You can also use a small sponge to apply paint, adding different colors to a single design, just as with a stencil brush. The finished effect depends on the type of sponge you use – ranging from the fine or coarse texture of a synthetic sponge to the random texture of a natural sponge.

1 Dab your sponge into paint (see p. 14) the consistency of light/single cream – neither too pastelike nor too watery. Apply it lightly to the stencil, using a stippling motion.

2 Rinse the sponge. When dry, apply a second color. Use a sponge that is just large enough to touch more than one cutout at a time, to create a mix of colors.

3 The end result shows the texture of the sponge. The touches of pink on the green leaves give them a lively, three-dimensional look (right).

PITFALLS

If you apply paint too thickly, using either a brush or a sponge, the effect is very solid and rather childish (near right). Test for excess paint on a piece of scrap paper. If you use too many colors at once and work them for too long, the result is muddy and heavy (far right).

Paint too thick

Too many colors

Stained Glass Effect

This effect is best achieved with a brush or sponge that is small enough to allow you to isolate a single area of the design and paint it individually. The stencil consists of thin lines, like the lead divisions in a stained glass window, and the result, especially if stenciled against a dark color, resembles stained glass work.

1 *Fix the stencil in place with repositioning glue/Spray Mount. Apply the first color to one area of your stencil – here, the flower – using the swirling technique. To prevent a buildup of paint along the bridges, apply paint mainly in the middle of each shape.*

2 *Apply a second color to the next area of your stencil – here, the background – using the swirling technique. Again, apply paint mainly in the center of each shape. As in stained glass work, the two colors should not blend into each other.*

3 *Use a slightly damp cloth to remove a little paint from the middle of each shape (above), leaving more paint at the edges. This gives the appearance of light coming through the stencil (right).*

Stippled and Wiped Chair

ABOVE *Three stencils were used on this chair – two flowers on the three back slats, and a border of leaves on the legs and front. Orange, pale yellow, and bright blue were applied in various combinations, using both the stippled and wiped techniques.*

Small Stippled Bowl

ABOVE *This wooden bowl was frottaged (see p. 13) in blue over terra-cotta. A simple design was then stenciled around the edge of the bowl, using the stippled and wiped methods.*

Soldier Cushion

RIGHT Two stencils were used on this plain blue cushion cover. The tree was printed in dark blue, then overprinted with white leaves. Strong, contrasting colors added dynamic accents to the soldier. The soldier's feet were used as a border in dark yellow.

COLOR COMBINATIONS

Olive-greens and ochers on deep terra-cotta

Fruit Tray

LEFT The wiped brush technique predominates on this stencil. The mix of colors gives the fruit a lively, three-dimensional look.

Blues and reds on off-white

Slightly muted clear colors on warm yellow

Fleur-de-lis Table

ABOVE AND BELOW A bit of the wood showing through the blue-gray basecoat of this table adds interest to the leaves and fleurs-de-lis stenciled in gray, green, blue, and deep red.

Metallic waxes on deep blue

Using Rollers

A ROLLER PROVIDES A quick way to stencil, especially over large areas such as walls and floors. It gives the stencil either a flat, solid look or a slightly speckled appearance, depending on how much paint and pressure you apply. Even with a traditional design, a roller tends to give the finished stencil a modern look. Stencils designed for use with a roller generally have larger holes, because the roller may miss parts of too small and intricate a design. It is easy to do a stencil in one color; but by carefully manipulating the roller, it is also possible to apply several colors at one time, using either the same roller or several different ones. The smaller the roller, the more manageable it will be.

Roller-stenciled Chest of Drawers
This design used olive-green, yellow ocher, and terra-cotta, randomly stenciled with a roller over the blue base on this small chest of drawers. The close-up detail shows how the texture was varied by rolling over parts of the leaves with the edge of the roller, making lines and thicker patches of paint in some areas.

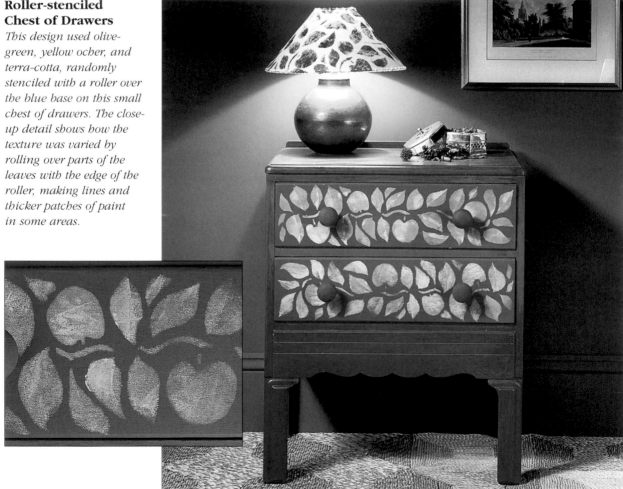

TOOLS & MATERIALS

Acetate stencil

Roller tray and roller

Paint

Paper for removing excess paint

Masking tape

Repositioning glue/Spray Mount

The Basic Technique

1 Load the roller with a little paint (see p. 14). If paint oozes from the sponge when you apply pressure to the roller on paper, you have too much paint. Remove the excess by rolling it on paper (left).

2 Fix the stencil in place (see p. 21). Apply the roller in an irregular pattern over areas of the design (below)

3 Apply a contrasting second color, in some places over the first color and in other places on its own. Most areas of the stencil should contain both colors to give it a three-dimensional, unified effect.

4 Partly remove the stencil (right) to check that the paint has gone on as required. Here, the roller was used to define the two sides of the leaves (inset).

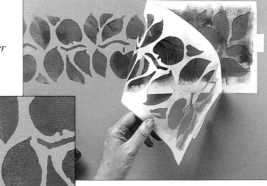

Varying Paint Thickness

1 *Fix the stencil (see p. 21) and roll lightly over it with the sponge roller and paint.*

2 *You can apply the paint thinly, using a roller containing a little, nearly dry, paint. This creates a light, speckled effect that lets your base color show through.*

3 *To create an even, opaque effect either apply two thin coats of paint or apply one thick coat using a roller saturated with paint or apply more pressure to the roller.*

Using Two Colors

1 *Put two colors in the tray, one on each side. Roll the sponge so that it picks up both colors.*

2 *Apply the roller to your stencil. Do not roll in too many directions, or the separate colors will merge together and become muddy.*

ALTERNATIVE

After you have completed your stencil (either with a single color, two colors applied separately as in *The Basic Technique* [see p. 45] or two colors applied at the same time as in *Using Two Colors* [left]), you can repeat the process by moving the stencil slightly. This allows you to apply an additional color deliberately off-register. The first coat should be fairly solid, with lighter pressure used for the top coat. Carefully done, this technique creates an unusual highlight for a design.

3 *Here, terra-cotta red on the right of the roller has colored the main section of the house, while olive green on the left of the roller has colored the ground. The left of the roller was also used to paint olive green on the roof.*

Stenciled Box

LEFT AND ABOVE A repeating design was stenciled in a dark neutral color onto the frottaged box (see p. 13). The stencil appears solid and even, in contrast to the bright textured background.

COLOR COMBINATIONS

Green-gray on blue

Brown on beige

Pale ocher on dark red

Blue and White Wall

ABOVE A roller was used lightly on most of this design – based on old Chinese wallpaper – to give a stippled effect. Below the chair rail, a roller was used with more pressure to create a stronger effect.

Blue-black on wood

PITFALLS

To prevent paint from seeping under your stencil (right), make sure the roller is not too wet (particularly after washing it) or overloaded with paint. Also, do not apply too much pressure to the roller.

Using Spray Paints

Spray-painting stencils is a fairly recent technique. It works especially well for delicate, detailed stencil designs. The spray reaches and perfectly defines the smallest and most intricate stencil cuts, which would probably be lost using the roller or brush techniques. Good for use on walls, spraying is also very effective on furniture, glass and fabric. The spray creates a myriad of fine dots of color, an effect that helps to retain the lightness and delicacy of a design. This technique is particularly suitable for beginners, although it may require some practice since it is tempting to over-spray, destroying the subtlety of the fine dots and turning the shapes into blocks of solid color.

**Spray-stenciled
Chest of Drawers**

This stencil was taken from a Japanese design but has been used in a random pattern on a white chest of drawers. The intricate, lacelike quality of the design is perfect for spray paint. In some areas the paint appears solid, in others light, giving the design a lively look.

TOOLS & MATERIALS

Acetate stencils

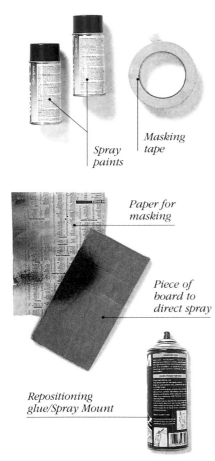

Spray paints

Masking tape

Paper for masking

Piece of board to direct spray

Repositioning glue/Spray Mount

The Basic Technique

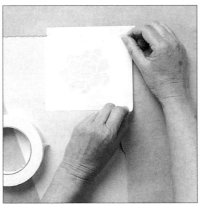

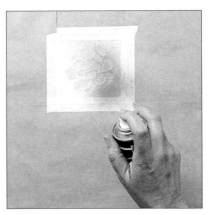

1 Fix the stencil in place using repositioning glue/Spray Mount to prevent the paint from seeping under the stencil. Tape masking paper all around the stencil.

2 Shake the can of spray paint well, then test it on some spare paper. Spray the stencil with a short burst of paint. A small amount of spray creates a delicate array of fine dots.

3 Apply the spray several times to one side of the stencil (inset), allowing the paint to dry for several seconds between each burst. After three or four sprays the paint is quite dense. The contrast between the well-defined shapes on the left and the softer, speckled effect on the right adds interest.

Multi-color Spraying

You can use several spray colors on a stencil to achieve a subtle effect. Blue and yellow in combination, for instance, will appear green from a distance. Be careful, however, not to spray too many colors, or to spray too heavily, or the effect will be muddy. Directing the spray at a piece of board, here corrugated cardboard, will ensure that only the lighter spray falls on the design.

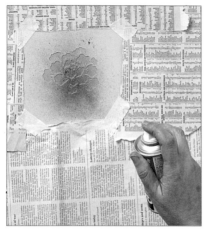

1 Fix and mask the stencil as in The Basic Technique (see p. 49). Spray lightly to give color all over, but spray more heavily in the center.

2 Lightly apply a second color. Use a piece of board to mask some of the first color and allow only excess spray to fall on the design.

3 Apply a third color. This time use the board mask to direct the paint toward the center of the flower and keep the color light.

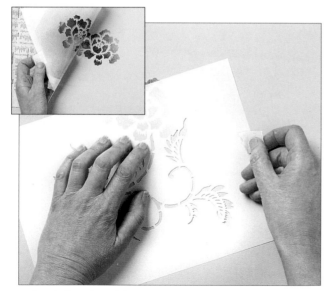

4 Lift the edge of the stencil to see if the color is working (inset) – if there is not enough of one particular color, replace the stencil and spray lightly again. When the flower is dry, place the leaf stencil next to it. You can see through a new or washed acetate stencil to position it accurately.

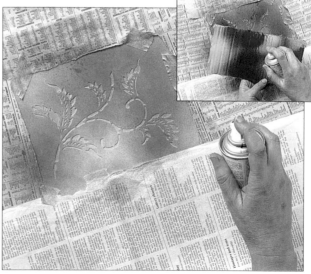

5 Mask around the stencil and spray your main color – here, green – lightly over the second stencil (above). To create depth, spray more densely in some areas than others. To coordinate with the flower, spray touches of the blue, yellow, and red over parts of the stencil (inset).

The Finished Design

Multi-color spraying gives a stencil design a sense of depth when viewed from afar (right). This comes from the delicate buildup of different colors that appear to merge when sprayed on. On closer inspection (below right) you can clearly see the variety of colors, and how the spray paint was used to highlight the delicacy of the design. The small spray dots are most apparent at the edges of the outer petals, while the center shows a denser effect.

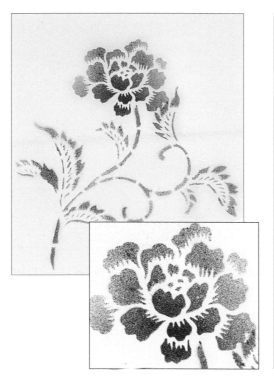

PITFALLS

If you do not hold the stencil down securely with repositioning glue/Spray Mount, the paint can easily seep under the design, resulting in a blurred image. If too much spray is used, it results in solid color, eliminating the fine dots that add depth and liveliness.

Spraying on Fabric

Because of the deep pile on velvet, it is easiest to make a stencil design on this fabric using the spray technique. Other techniques may leave a thick coat of paint on the surface, flattening the pile, but spray paint does not. Although the paint is quite sturdy and withstands light washing or dry cleaning (a cushion sprayed ten years ago is now faded), it does not last indefinitely.

1 Lightly secure the fabric to a flat surface with masking tape, so that it is smooth and wrinkle-free, but not stretched.

2 Secure the stencil carefully to the velvet, using repositioning glue/Spray Mount. Spray-paint the stencil as described in Multi-color Spraying *(see p. 50).*

3 The movement of the pile of the velvet can change the effect of the design. At times, some colors will seem to disappear, while others look stronger.

Spraying on Glass

Sprays are more effective for stenciling on glass than brushes, sponges, or rollers, because they create an evenly adhering coat. Stenciled glass must always be cleaned carefully since strong abrasives will remove the paint. For a longlasting effect spray on the inside surface of windows, or glass objects.

1 Position the stencil on the glass, using repositioning glue/Spray Mount, then mask the area all round with paper and masking tape.

2 Spray the stencil as in The Basic Technique *(see p. 49). Here, green was used first, strongly in places and more lightly in others.*

3 Apply a second color – here, yellow – in patches. In some areas, use equal measures of the two colors to make a lighter green.

4 Check the color (above) and spray again, if necessary. The finished effect (right) is quite solid, and not easy to see through. A less dense, lighter colored spray would create a semi-transparent effect.

Candle Holder

LEFT *A very small stencil was used on the outside of this glass globe (the stencil has to be tiny to accommodate the curve of the glass). Because masking can be a laborious process, you may want to position several stencils at the same time to accomplish more in one spraying.*

Red Lacquer Chair

BELOW This modern pine chair was sprayed a deep red. Chinese-style designs – figures, pagodas, and trees interspersed with latticework – were then stenciled on in deep gold and bright warm yellow spray paint.

COLOR COMBINATIONS

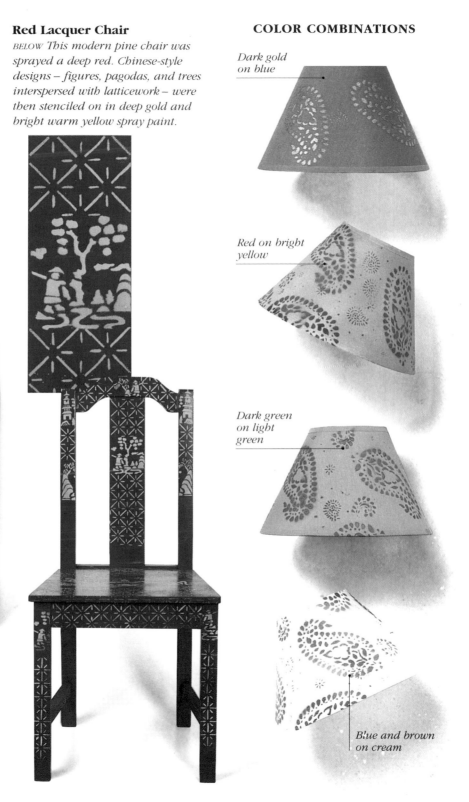

Dark gold on blue

Red on bright yellow

Dark green on light green

Blue and brown on cream

Velvet Curtain

ABOVE This brown velvet curtain has been stenciled with a design inspired by styles of the 1920s, when velvet printed with flowing abstract designs, often in neutral colors, was especially popular.

Hand Painting with Stencils

Hand-painted Tray
This tray was painted deep terra-cotta and stenciled with a flower posy design. Spots, dashes, and lines were then hand painted on, to give a cool, elegant, yet country-style effect.

I N THE PAST, stencils were sometimes used as a backdrop for a design, over which hand painting was done. Hand painting may sound daunting, but it does not require any great skill. You can transform a flower stencil, for instance, simply by adding spots, dashes, swirls, and lines. The hand painting added to the floral stencil in *The Basic Technique* (see p. 55), makes the design look more naturalistic. You can vary a repeated design, in that way making it look slightly different and individual each time. Two other hand-painting techniques use the stencil as a template, either drawing around or filling in with gold size before brushing bronze powder on top.

TOOLS & MATERIALS

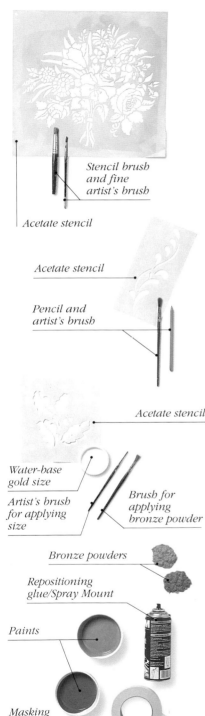

Stencil brush
and fine
artist's brush

Acetate stencil

Acetate stencil

Pencil and
artist's brush

Acetate stencil

Water-base
gold size

Artist's brush
for applying
size

Brush for
applying
bronze powder

Bronze powders

Repositioning
glue/Spray Mount

Paints

Masking
tape

The Basic Technique

1 Use a stencil brush to stencil the bunch of flowers (see p. 39), so that each part of the design can be done in a separate color.

2 Using a fine artist's brush, define the petals and leaves with lines and spots of paint (see p. 15). Here, dark lines were used on the lighter colors (inset) and off-white on the darker colors.

Using Bronze Powders

You use bronze powders – fine, metallic powders – over a special glue called gold size. This is a traditional technique that was popular on early American furniture. It works particularly well on dark colors.

1 Fix the stencil in place. With an artist's brush, apply the water-base gold size inside the stencil shape. Be careful not to allow the size to seep under the stencil.

2 When the size has turned clear, put a little bronze powder on an unsized place, then brush the powder lightly onto the size. Here, two colors were used to give added interest.

3 Allow the design to set for several hours, then brush off the excess powder by wiping gently over the work with a slightly damp sponge (right). Varnish it with oil-base varnish (see p. 16) to protect the bronze powders.

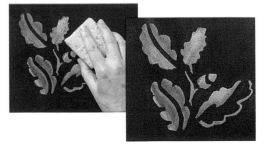

Using the Stencil as a Template

A stencil is used as a guide for hand painting on much traditional painted furniture, particularly on folkwork. The stencil acts as a template to create a consistent design. The traced areas are then hand painted with an artist's brush to give the stencil design a slightly irregular look.

1 Secure the stencil, then draw around each shape in the design with a sharp pencil. You may need a piece of string to act as a guideline for a border.

2 Continue the design, making it into a border. A transparent acetate stencil allows you to see the pencil design clearly.

3 With an artist's brush, apply green paint (see p. 14) within the lines and shapes. Paint each line in one movement, pressing down to make it wider and releasing to make it finer.

4 With a fine-pointed artist's brush, paint a line in dark green on the right-hand bottom of each leaf to create a shadow effect.

5 On the top and left-hand side of each leaf, paint a light green line as a highlight (inset). There is a convention in hand painting that the light always comes from the top left-hand side.

Folkstyle Crib

RIGHT This charming crib was inspired by Eastern European folk painting. Strong, predominantly primary colors were used on the stencil.

Indian-style Stool

ABOVE AND RIGHT An Indian-inspired stencil of a horse with other abstract designs was used on this stool. These were enhanced by hand painting.

Chicken Canister

ABOVE The dark blue roosters and hens were highlighted with dots and lines in cream paint.

Chinese-style Panel

LEFT The stencils on this panel were enhanced with spirals, dots, swirls, and dashes that echo hand-painted Chinese wallpapers.

COLOR COMBINATIONS

Green, blue-green shadows, and yellow-green highlights on dark yellow

Middle-blue, dark blue shadows, and pale blue highlights on blue

Middle-brown, dark brown shadows, and off-white highlights on beige

Heraldic Bedhead

ABOVE AND RIGHT The folk-art motif on this gray-blue headboard was decorated with lines and spots in various colors.

Dark yellow, gray-brown shadows, and off-white highlights on dark red

Reverse Stenciling

Reverse-stenciled Mantelpiece

This mantelpiece has been reverse-stenciled in blue and a light gray-brown over an olive-green base. The sides were deliberately made softer than the center and top edge, to create a strong central focus.

A STENCIL NORMALLY CONSISTS of the holes cut in poster board or acetate. In this stenciling technique it is the reverse: a shape is cut out of the poster board or acetate, and instead of discarding this central shape, you use it as the stencil. Reverse stencils act like silhouettes or shadow puppets. With ordinary stencils many shapes often make up the design, but a reverse stencil generally consists of just one complete shape. You can use any stenciling method with reverse stencils. The spray method works well for intricate shapes, such as delicate ferns. The roller method is speedier for large areas; it also gives a solid effect more easily.

TOOLS & MATERIALS

Roller tray and roller

Craft knife

Paintbrush

Paint

Poster board stencil

Masking fluid

Brush for applying masking fluid

Repositioning glue/Spray Mount

The Basic Technique

The method chosen for applying the paint is up to you. Roller stenciling (see pp. 44–47) has been used here because it is the quickest technique, and because it most easily makes a solid contrast to the silhouette design.

1 Fix the stencil in place with repositioning glue/Spray Mount. Roll paint (see p. 14) over the design in all directions, taking care not to use too much paint.

2 When the paint is dry, remove the stencil. You may need to use a sharp implement to lift it. Reposition the stencil and roll the paint on to meet the paint already applied.

3 Continue in this way. Or flip the stencil over (when dry) so that the design faces in the opposite direction. If you apply paint lightly around the stencil, it will give less contrast to the design.

4 When the first coat is dry, use the roller to apply another layer of paint all over the design. Here, a warm beige was used to help soften the rather hard outlines of the stencil. If you are combining less contrasting colors, this step may not be necessary.

Using Leaves

Several different types of real fern leaves were used here. You can also use other leaves, such as oak or maple. Leaves are fragile and break easily so get a good selection before starting. Use spray paint (see pp. 48–53) with leaves; the spray will define even the most delicate shapes.

1 Fix the leaves securely in place using repositioning glue/Spray Mount. Direct most of the spray at a piece of board so that the leaves do not become sodden with paint.

2 Allow the paint to dry for a few minutes. Remove the leaves, being careful not to break them. You can reuse them several times before they become too heavy with paint.

3 Rearrange the leaves, placing them partly on the sprayed background and partly over the other leaf shapes. Spray with a second color.

4 The finished effect has different levels of opacity. Where there are two colors the effect will be more opaque than where there is just one color.

Repeat Borders

Reverse stencils are particularly good for making a border. Instead of applying the paint all round the stencil, you apply it only to one side. Any technique will work, but the wiped brush technique (see p. 39) gives the greatest texture and vitality.

1 Fix the stencil in position, then mark out a border line above and below with masking tape, leaving a little space around the stencil. Apply the paint outward in light brushstrokes.

2 Remove and reposition the stencil about 1in/ 2.5cm away from the first stencil position. Brush paint on in the same direction as for the first stencil.

3 *Continue with the design, leaving a gap of the same size each time and always brushing the paint outward. Stencil color into the gap between the masking tape lines to give a well-defined edge to the design.*

4 *Remove the masking tape. The border will contain a series of overlapping leaves, whose color will vary in density. The brushmarks may go right over the base color, or the base color may show through, as here.*

Using Sticky Labels

A stationery store is a good source of sticky labels, which make excellent reverse stencils. Stars, stripes, circles, rectangles, letters, and numbers of different sizes make easy, lighthearted abstract and geometric patterns. Test them first, to make sure the adhesive does not remove the paint on your surface.

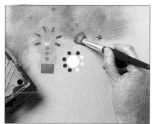

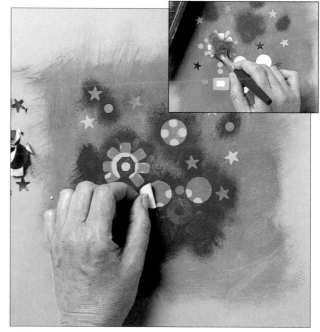

1 *Make an arrangement of stickers. Use a craft knife to position the stickers accurately, especially the very small ones.*

2 *Apply the paint (see p. 14) all over the stickers. The brush method was used here, but you can also use spray paint or a roller.*

3 *Remove the stickers, using a craft knife to help lift them, if necessary. You may be able to reuse some of the stickers.*

4 *Apply more stickers to the design. Put some over the painted area and others over the sticker areas already formed.*

5 *Brush a second color over the new stickers (inset). You can paint over the whole area or, as here, just over the second batch of stickers. Remove the stickers. You should now have three colors, including the basecoat.*

Using Masking Fluid

Masking fluid is normally used as a means of blocking out areas in watercolor painting, but you can also use it to make a reverse stencil. It resembles a liquid rubber/rubber cement and dries hard when you paint it on a surface. It can take up to several hours to dry, especially when you paint it on thickly, but the thicker you paint it, the easier it is to peel off later and the better the effect.

Stickered Lamp

LEFT The cream base was covered with round stickers and painted blue. After more stickers were added it was painted orange and all the stickers were removed, revealing the colors beneath. Blue was applied between strips of masking tape on the orange shade.

1 Fix the stencil in position using masking tape. Draw around the design with a sharp pencil. Here, the design was drawn on wood, but you could also do it on a painted surface.

2 Remove the stencil and paint a generous layer of masking fluid onto the shapes. Paint right up to the pencil marks, so that you cover them with the fluid.

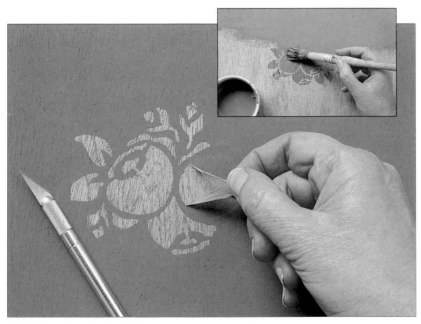

3 When dry, the fluid becomes transparent. Cover your whole surface with a little paint (see p. 14), using a bristle brush (inset). When the paint is dry, pick up a bit of the dried masking fluid, with a craft knife, and peel it off.

Silhouette Box

ABOVE Reverse stencils were made using enlarged photocopies from a book of silhouettes. These were then stenciled on the side of a box using the roller method.

Stickered Table

LEFT AND BELOW A few stickers of numbers and letters were applied to the cream base of this table. The tabletop was then painted warm red and the sides and legs gray-blue. More stickers were then applied and painted over in beige before being removed.

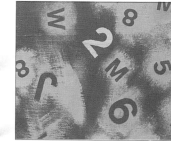

COLOR COMBINATIONS

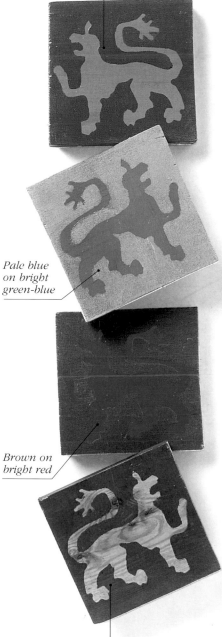

Dark terra-cotta on pale terra-cotta

Pale blue on bright green-blue

Brown on bright red

Blue on varnished wood

Leaf Lampshade

LEFT This green fabric lampshade was sprayed with deep red paint over real fern leaves. The leaves were lifted and repositioned, then random patches of green spray were applied.

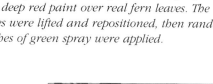

Silhouette and Leaf Table

LEFT AND ABOVE The silhouette of a tree was made into a reverse stencil. Oak leaf and acorn shapes were used around the outside of the central oval on this long table.

Stamping

Tools and Materials

Felt-tip pen

Sharp craft knife

Pencil

TODAY YOU CAN BUY numerous ready-made stamps, sometimes called blocks. You can also easily cut and make stamps yourself using household materials such as Styrofoam/polystyrene (from packing cases or packaged food), synthetic sponges, foam rubber, or even potatoes (right). You can use nail heads, corks, paper cups, and plastic bubble wrap (below), and experiment with other items to make different shapes. Similarly, there are many different rollers, both plain and patterned, that you can buy (below right), but you can also cut your own patterns into sponge rollers to make your own unique designs.

Designing Stamps

ABOVE For drawing on and cutting potatoes, Styrofoam/polystyrene, sponge, and corrugated cardboard, you need a pencil, the strong, positive line of a felt-tip pen, and a sharp craft knife.

Making Guidelines

RIGHT This apparatus contains powdered chalk, either white or colored. You pull the string out of the container to make straight guidelines. Then, by pulling the string taut and plucking it, you leave a chalky print.

Chalk line

Using Found Objects

BELOW AND RIGHT You can use all these household objects for stamping, and make delightful instant patterns of circles, lines, and dots, or create pictures.

Precut novelty sponge

Precut novelty sponge

Corrugated paper

Nails with large heads

Cork

Eraser

Cotton swabs

Paper cup

Strips of corrugated cardboard

Bubble wrap

Making Stamps

BELOW AND RIGHT You can use readily available materials such as potatoes, Styrofoam/polystyrene, and sponges for stamping. You can easily cut them with a large, sharp household knife and shape them into designs using a sharp craft knife.

Large, sharp, household knife

Thin Styrofoam/polystyrene

Potatoes

Sponge

Styrofoam/polystyrene taken from packaging

Mounting Stamps

BELOW Mounting your designs on wooden blocks makes it easier to handle them. A knob is not essential, but makes handling even easier.

Wooden block with a corrugated cardboard design on it

Back of wooden block, with a knob

Wood glue for sticking down the design

Using Rollers

BELOW AND RIGHT There are many types of rollers available in hardware and paint supply stores. You can buy them in various widths and patterns; there are even rollers that have a container for paint and two plain rollers, which apply paint evenly and continually to a patterned rubber roller.

Large sponge roller divided by an elastic band

Patterned roller with a container for paint and two plain rollers

Hard sponge roller with pattern already cut

Elastic bands

Small roller and tray

Designing Stamps

Stamp Sources

Fabrics, china, tiles, and books are all good sources of stamp designs. For the simplest shapes, try a potato stamp. You can also make simple shapes out of sponge, but to create more complicated shapes, use Styrofoam/polystyrene.

YOU CAN TURN many designs that are unsuitable for a stencil into a stamp. Stamps allow great flexibility of design, from broad shapes to fine, intricate patterns. While you cannot reverse a stamp to make the design face in both directions, as you can a stencil, you can incorporate long, thin tendrils and circles within circles, without having to use bridges. The material you use to make the stamp will dictate how intricate you can make your design. A potato is good for basic designs with little detail, but by the second day it will dry out and start shrinking. A sponge has a finer surface and can take more detail, but for intricate designs you can use Styrofoam/polystyrene, although even the finest Styrofoam/polystyrene gives a degree of texture to your design. Strong corrugated cardboard is probably best of all for making intricate and long-lasting designs. Its only drawback is that cutting it out can be a laborious process.

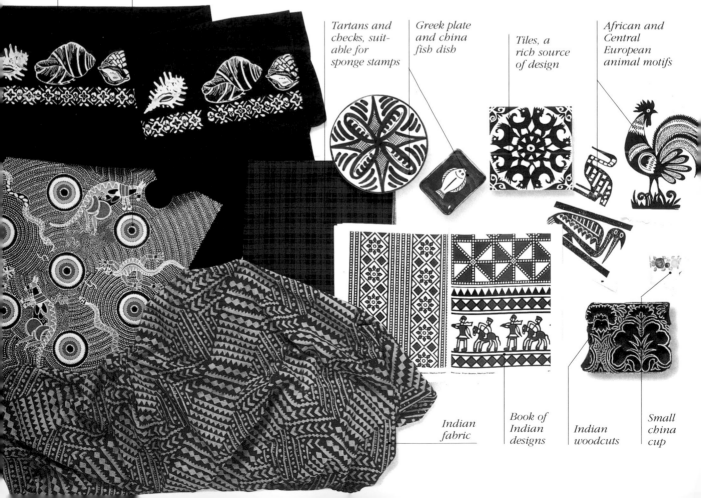

Fabric design

Australian Aborigine design

Tartans and checks, suitable for sponge stamps

Greek plate and china fish dish

Tiles, a rich source of design

African and Central European animal motifs

Indian fabric

Book of Indian designs

Indian woodcuts

Small china cup

Making a Stamp

While it is relatively easy to make a stamp, it takes time and requires concentration. You may find that corrugated paper is easier to cut than corrugated cardboard, although it has a greater tendency to

break up. You can make your stamp easier to handle by mounting it on a block of wood. Attach a wooden door knob to the back of your block to make a handle (see p. 67).

1 Using a tile (or other) design from a source book, trace the shape, and then transfer it to a piece of corrugated cardboard or corrugated paper, using a soft pencil and tracing paper (see p. 29). You can simplify the design, if necessary, so there are not too many complicated shapes.

2 With a sharp craft knife, cut the design out carefully. If you use corrugated paper and it breaks up, do not worry. The broken parts of the design can be stuck back together on the block.

3 Take a block of wood, slightly larger than the design. Attach a wooden door knob to the back as a handle. Or simply handle the block from the sides.

4 Apply a white wood glue to the front of the block, spreading it evenly all over the surface.

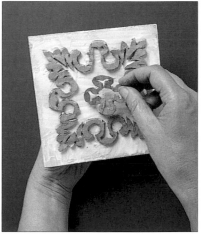

5 Stick the largest piece of the design down first and finish with the smallest. Complete the stamp by applying a thin layer of wood glue all over the design and sides to protect it.

Stamping on a Stamped Background

To add variety, you can create a base pattern on your surface, then stamp over it with another design. You can create regular overstamping, such as the symmetrical tile pattern shown below, or an overall pattern (right) that is made up of two different patterns combined.

1 Mount some bubble wrap on a piece of wooden board to make a sturdy printing block. Cover the surface of the bubble wrap with water-base paint.

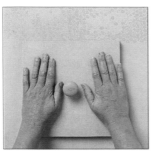

2 While the paint is still wet, press the block down firmly on your surface, applying an even pressure all over.

3 Roll water-base paint onto your stamp, covering the whole surface well. Print three or four times on scrap paper until the stamp begins to print clearly. Roll on fresh paint each time you stamp.

4 Print the stamp on the surface already painted, applying an even pressure to it. Use a string guideline to keep the design straight.

5 Here, the stamp with its symmetrical design (right) was printed to resemble tiles, leaving a similar-size gap between each tile shape. The corrugated paper of the stamp shows up as irregularly printed stripes.

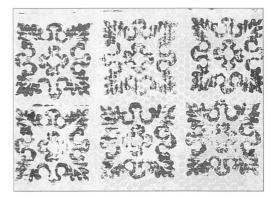

Double Stamping

1 Paint an irregular sponge with water-base paint. Spread the paint thoroughly. Test on some scrap paper.

2 Print the sponge on a painted surface. Here, the sponge was printed to resemble bricks.

3 Roll paint all over your stamp. Test on some scrap paper to check the print and how it repeats.

4 *Print the stamp on your prepared surface. Here, the stamp was printed where three brick patterns from the previous sponge stamp join.*

5 *The finished print (right) has an overall pattern and the uneven printing is enhanced by the traditional design and colors.*

Etching Styrofoam/Polystyrene

This technique was originally adapted from metal etching, which uses speciality equipment. All you need here is a thin piece of Styrofoam/polystyrene, a felt-tip pen, a pencil, some water-base paint, and a roller. By pressing down on the pencil you incise the design into the Styrofoam/polystyrene.

1 *Lightly sketch your design, here a stylized bird, with a felt-tip pen on the Styrofoam/polystyrene.*

2 *Using a pencil, incise the design into the Styrofoam/polystyrene to a depth of about ⅛in/3mm.*

3 *Roll paint evenly and thoroughly over the entire design.*

4 *Test the stamp on scrap paper. Keep adding paint to make an even print.*

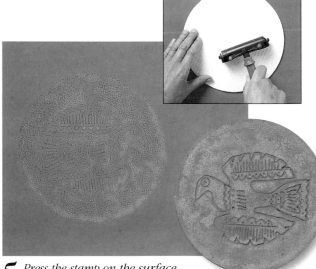

5 *Press the stamp on the surface to be printed, rolling over the back of the stamp with a craft roller sold for linoleum printing (inset), or a sponge roller. The pencil lines do not print but let the base color show through.*

Using Found Objects

Stamped Cupboard

This small kitchen cupboard was painted deep terra-cotta. Green paint on the rim of a paper cup was stamped on the cabinet to make semicircles. Off-white dots of paint on a cork were applied in between.

THERE IS GREAT FUN to be had from finding objects around the house with which to create stamp designs. Paper cups and lids of various sizes stamp thin, uneven circles, which you can use as arcs or chains. You can make stamped spots and dots with a range of household items, from pencil ends to cotton swabs. Stamping with hard objects, such as the heads of nails, tends to leave a fairly heavy layer of paint and a rough, uneven texture when dry. Try stamping with string, the end of a clothes pin, or a rubber ball. And every child knows that a hand print works extremely well!

TOOLS & MATERIALS

Roller tray and
water-base paints

Brushes for
applying paint
to stamps

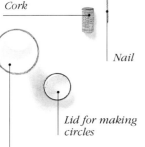

Corrugated
paper

Bubble
wrap of
different
sizes

Cork

Nail

Lid for making
circles

Paper cup for
making circles

The Basic Technique

*1 Having created a guide-
line using a piece of
string attached with some
mounting putty/Blu-Tack
(see p. 35), apply water-
base paint to the cork.*

*2 To stamp, press the
cork down firmly. Test
the pressure and how much
paint you need before you
begin. Too much of either
causes paint to ooze from
the sides, ruining the shape.*

*3 Coat a large-headed
nail with paint and
stamp with it. It is usual to
add paint after each stamping, but test both cork and
nail to see how often you
need to reapply the paint.*

*4 Corrugated paper is often
used for packaging. You
can cut it into squares, paint
it (inset), then stamp in
diamond shapes using
alternate colors and
stamping in alternate
directions (right). Do
not press too hard or the
corrugated ridges will
squash and obliterate
the painted lines.*

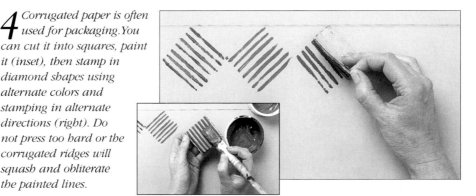

*5 To make a semicircle use a length of
string as a guideline with a piece of
paper on one side of it. Paint the rim of the
paper cup and press it in place (above).
Paint a square-shaped lipstick lid and use
it as a stamp inside the semicircles (inset).*

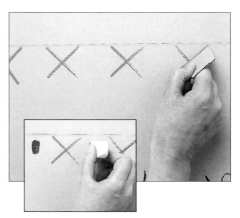

*6 Use a small, cut piece of corrugated
cardboard to make crosses or lines
(above). Use the end of an eraser in
between the crosses to make a softly
rounded rectangle (inset).*

Stamping a Picture

Abstract border patterns are not the only use for decorative stamping with found objects. Here, some bubble wrap, corrugated cardboard, corrugated paper, a cork, a paper cup, a lid, and a nail were used to create a picture that could be applied to a panel or picture frame, as shown opposite.

1 Lightly paint the surface of the bubble wrap, so that the paint appears only on the circles. Press down evenly to create cloudy sky.

2 Using a rectangle of corrugated paper painted green, press down evenly to make a field.

3 Paint a cut piece of corrugated paper, then stamp to give vertical lines that look like grass or trees.

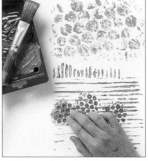

4 Cut out circles of bubble wrap with smaller-size bubbles, and stamp in orange or a similar color to represent fruit trees.

5 With the edge of some corrugated cardboard, stamp the trunks of the trees. Allow the card to bend a little so that the lines are not too rigid.

6 Use a cork to stamp shrubs at the foot of the trees. Stamp several together, and one on top of another in places, to resemble foliage.

7 Use the rim of a paper cup and the small lid of a pot to indicate the sun (inset top). Stamp several times, each time slightly further to one side, to create the effect of shimmering light. Use a small nail head to define flowers on the shrubs (inset bottom).

8 Stamping with found objects is most effective when used to create relatively simple scenes, such as this landscape. To vary the effect, try experimenting with any number of objects.

Aboriginal-style Table

LEFT AND BELOW The design on this table was inspired by Australian Aboriginal work. The table was painted terra-cotta, then a large nail head was used to stamp the dots. This produced an uneven surface so the tabletop was rubbed down with sandpaper, giving it a slightly worn look.

COLOR COMBINATIONS

Red lines and blue spots on middle-green

Blue-gray lines and red spots on green-blue

Gray lines and dark red spots on brown

Blue lines and brown and beige spots on white

Blue and White Frame

LEFT This frame was painted a cool blue, then off-white dots were added, using a nail head and a cotton swab as stamps. White paint was applied along the rims using the edge of some corrugated cardboard.

Picture Frame

RIGHT Bubble wrap, corrugated cardboard, and erasers of various sizes were used to decorate this frame.

Making Stamps

S TAMPS, SOMETIMES CALLED printing blocks, make attractive patterns on
walls and furniture. Many cultures – particularly those of India, Africa,
and Indonesia – have decorated with stamps, usually ones carved out
of wood. Stamps were also used to make early wallpapers and fabrics.
Today you can buy printing stamps, but you can also easily make them using
readily available materials such as sponges, Styrofoam/polystyrene, and
potatoes. You can make many designs with stamps that you cannot make
with ordinary stencils. The simplest and longest-lasting stamp material is the
synthetic sponge. Its texture is finely granular, and it works well on walls
and furniture. Simply wash the sponge out after each use and let it dry.
Alternatively the potato stamp has a random, uneven texture.

TOOLS & MATERIALS

Large, sharp knife for cutting sponge

Synthetic sponge cut into pieces

Water-base paint and brush for applying it to stamp

Second color and brush for applying it to stamp

Masking tape (optional)

Felt-tip pen

The Basic Technique

1 Cut a large sponge into rectangles, using a sharp knife. This is easy to do if the sponge is dry and new and the knife is sharp.

2 Coat the surface of the dry sponge with a layer of water-base paint. You can paint this on with a brush or press the sponge onto a roller tray.

3 Start in a corner and work along the straight edge of a ceiling or, as here, create a straight edge using masking tape. If necessary, mark guidelines in pencil to keep the work regular. Recoat the sponge every time, or every second time.

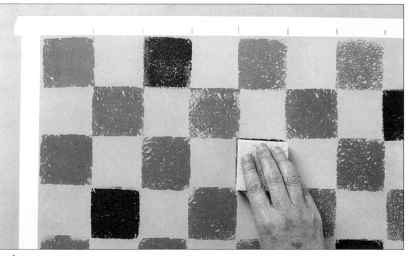

4 Overstamping – stamping a second color over the dry first color – can give an interesting effect and texture. It allows a little of the first color to show through.

ALTERNATIVES

Stamping with sponges allows great variety with little effort. You can use sponges to make checks (bottom) or other geometric designs (right and below). Using a very sharp craft knife, you can also create more intricate patterns, including curves, or shapes that appeal especially to children, such as ducks and cars.

A diamond and a triangle make up a border design.

This border is made of different-sized squares and a long rectangle. The thin outline is made by stamping with the edge of a cut sponge.

Over a pale blue background, alternating dark blue and pale brown squares were stamped. On the blue squares small dark and pale brown squares were randomly stamped.

A grid was made by stamping large squares with a small gap in between them. Smaller squares were stamped in the center and around the edge of each square.

Three shades of green were stamped over a middle-green. A potato stamp was applied to the center of every alternate square (see opposite).

Potato Stamping

Potatoes make an excellent stamping material because they are readily available and easy to use, though your design will be limited to the size and shape of the potato. A potato stamp block survives over the course of a day, but will be dry and unusable by the second day.

1 Using a large, sharp knife, halve the potato. A clean, regular cut will help give even printing. Dab the surface of the potato with absorbent paper to remove excess moisture.

2 Draw your design on the surface, using a felt-tip pen. Do not use a design that is too intricate.

3 Using a craft knife, cut into the potato along your lines (above). Then cut in from the sides to meet these lines. The unwanted part of the potato should fall away (inset).

4 When you have removed all the unwanted potato, and the design stands clear, paint the potato's surface. The water-base paint should be free-flowing but not watery.

5 Test the stamp on paper. You may need to recut some areas to sharpen the contours. If you do not apply enough pressure the stamp will appear weak.

6 Decide how you want your pattern to repeat before you stamp. Then stamp the design, using pressure from above to get a good print.

PITFALLS

If you use too much paint the edges of the design become blurred. With potato stamping in particular, the potato is in danger of sliding and distorting the design.

Paint too wet or done with a wet sponge

Potato has slipped, so design is blurred

Too much paint, so design has filled in

Stamping with Styrofoam/Polystyrene

Because large sheets of Styrofoam/polystyrene are often used in packaging, this material allows you to make a sizeable design. It is easy to cut patterns and quite intricate shapes in Styrofoam/polystyrene, and it produces a fairly regular granular-textured surface. The stamp will last for some time, although after a year or so the remaining paint seems to soften the design.

1   Using a very sharp knife, cut a block of Styrofoam/polystyrene out of a larger piece.

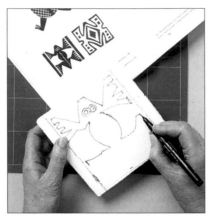

2   Copy your design onto the surface using a felt-tip pen. If you are unsure of your drawing skills, trace an enlarged photocopy.

3   With a sharp craft knife, cut out the design. Use a technique similar to that used in Step 3 of Potato Stamping (see p. 79).

4   Apply water-base paint using a roller. The firmness of the Styrofoam/polystyrene gives the roller a good surface for accepting the paint.

5   Press down firmly on the back of the Styrofoam/polystyrene (inset), making certain that the entire design prints. The print will have a delightful grainy texture (right).

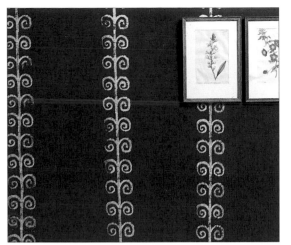

Styrofoam/ Polystyrene- stamped Wall

LEFT An indigo-blue background was stamped with a design cut out of Styrofoam/ polystyrene, using white paint. The design was stamped in vertical stripes, using a weighted piece of string as a guide to keep it straight.

COLOR COMBINATIONS

Gray on dark red

Dark red and yellow ocher on bright blue

Styrofoam/Polystyrene- stamped Wooden Bowl

RIGHT This wooden bowl from a Moroccan market was stamped twice, first with a Styrofoam/polystyrene stamp of a bird, then with a border around the edges using pieces of Styrofoam/polystyrene. When dry, the bowl was waxed and polished to give it a soft sheen.

White on terra-cotta

Potato-stamped Cupboard

LEFT On the inner panels and drawer front of this cupboard, a roughly repeating pattern of dia- monds and rectangles was used in terra-cotta over a deep yellow.

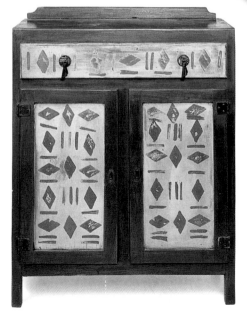

Gray-green and yellow ocher on bright green

Making Cylinder Stamps with Rollers

Roller-stamped Desk

Horizontal and vertical lines were made in terra-cotta, using a medium-width roller, over a yellow background. A small roller was cut down to make the thin blue lines which complete this tartan effect.

ROLLERS ARE A RELATIVELY modern painting tool, yet they were traditionally used as a method of applying pattern in the wallpaper industry, where they replaced block printing. You can use plain rollers to make stripes, checks, plaids, and tartans. By cutting or tying sponge rollers you can obtain different widths. And by using stripes of different widths you can create an enormous range of patterns. Look as well for ready-made patterned rollers or create your own pattern by cutting a design into a sponge roller. As an alternative consider a roller "machine," which makes a pattern on the wall using a patterned rubber roller.

TOOLS & MATERIALS

Roller tray,
paint, and
roller

Large roller,
tied with an
elastic band

Small roller,
tied with an
elastic band

Pencil

Water-base
paints

Chalk line

The Basic Technique

1 Paint the entire wall using a large roller. Two or more coats may be necessary, depending on the color chosen and the color you are covering.

2 Make a horizontal guideline using a chalk line (see p. 21). Fix the string close to the wall, then pluck it firmly to leave a line of chalk.

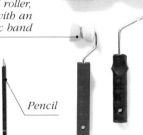

3 Use the roller width to gauge the height of the next chalk line down. Make a pencil mark at both ends of the wall to identify where to position the chalk line.

4 Continue making horizontal guidelines all the way down the wall. Here, they are an equal distance apart, but they need not be.

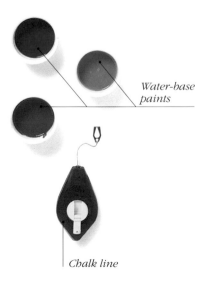

5 Load the roller with water-base paint and test on scrap paper (see p. 45). Apply to the wall in horizontal stripes, using the chalk lines as guides.

6 When dry, use a chalk line to make more guidelines vertically over the paint and background and print vertical lines in the same way.

Using an Elastic Band

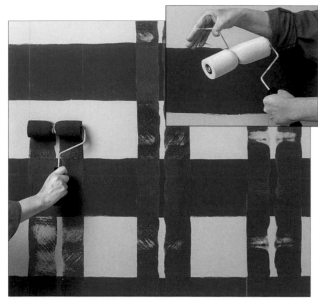

1 Divide a roller in two by winding string or an elastic band around the sponge (inset). Print with the roller in vertical stripes on the wall (above), using more or less paint to make a stronger or slightly uneven line.

2 Take a small roller and wind string or an elastic band around it, as before. Then make thin double lines, both vertically and horizontally, using the yellow squares as guidelines and keeping the double lines to one side.

Roller Patterns

There are many ready-made patterned rollers available at hardware and paint supply stores. The two shown here, in the center and on the far right, are made of hard sponge and rubber. They are intended for use with plaster, to make textured wall finishes. If you roll them in paint, however, you can create interesting effects on both walls and furniture. The small roller on the left was made by cutting geometric shapes into a sponge roller.

Small sponge roller, cut with a knife

Firm sponge roller, bought precut

Rubber roller, for making small spots

Cutting Patterns in Rollers

A patterned roller is used for the large-scale manufacture of wallpaper and fabrics. But you can create your own patterned roller by cutting a design into a sponge roller. To keep the sponge firm and achieve a reasonable print, keep your design simple and do not remove too much sponge.

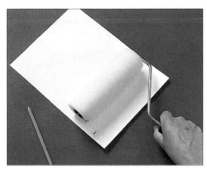

1 Place a sponge roller on a sheet of paper. Make a pencil mark on both the sponge and the paper at the point where the roller first touches the paper.

2 Roll the roller along the paper until the pencil mark on the sponge touches the paper again. Mark the paper at this point. This gives you the height of your design.

3 Draw your design to height on paper, making large, separate shapes. Leave a gap of 1in/2.5cm at the top and bottom, so that your design does not repeat too closely.

4 Cut the shapes of the design out of the paper using a craft knife. You will be left with a stencil.

5 Attach the paper stencil to the roller, using masking tape. This is quite difficult, and you may need the help of a friend.

8 Load the patterned roller with water-base paint, so the sponge is saturated but not dripping. Test on some spare paper. Do not roll over a printed motif twice; it is difficult to achieve an accurate overprint. Cover the roller often with paint to make sure that the pattern prints well.

6 Fill in the stencil with a little dry paint. Remove the stencil to leave the design visible on the roller.

7 Using a craft knife, cut out the design, as in Step 3 of Potato Stamping (see p. 79). You can make a positive or negative shape.

Using a Patterned Roller

Patterned rollers have been used for a long time as a means of making patterns on walls. The rollers come in several widths and many different patterns.

If you use them over striped, plain, or textured backgrounds, different colors can make the same design appear dramatic or soft and classic.

1 Pour water-base paint into the container below the patterned roller. The paint should flow easily.

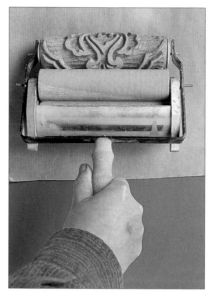

3 Test roll on some scrap paper stuck to the wall. Make sure the paint spreads all over the rubber roller and that you have the correct vertical holding position.

4 Starting at the bottom of the wall, move upward, keeping the roller machine at the same vertical angle.

2 Replace the two metal rollers. The paint is applied evenly to these and then to the patterned rubber roller.

5 For the next row, start at the bottom again, carefully aligning the pattern with the row already completed. This is probably the most difficult part of the process.

6 The finished wall (right) has a delightful handmade quality. A gap will remain all around the wall of about 1–2in/2.5–5cm, where the roller cannot reach.

Dotted Wooden Box

RIGHT Using a patterned roller, a strong blue was applied over a deep orange basecoat. When dry, small dots were applied in pale yellow using a dotted roller.

Striped Flower Pot

LEFT Stripes were applied in alternate green and red over white. Using a small hand-cut roller, a pattern was then added in blue paint.

COLOR COMBINATIONS

Red and green on blue

Vertical Striped Wall

LEFT Two rollers were used to create this effect, one with a rich brown-red and the other with a deep yellow ocher. The stripes were applied alternately, before the paint was completely dry, so the colors merged into each other, creating a soft edge.

Brown and white on blue

Yellow and blue on green

Dark red, yellow, and orange on purple

Horizontal Striped Wall

ABOVE Several layers of color were applied to this wall, beginning with dark blue and ending with a paler blue. The two horizontal lines were made using a small roller at the top and a similar roller cut in half below.

Combining Techniques

EACH OF THE TECHNIQUES shown in this book results in a different texture and effect. By combining two or three techniques you can give designs on walls and furniture added depth and interest. The stenciling techniques have a neater, more predictable and controlled appearance than the stamped techniques, which give a rougher, more textured and uneven paint surface. In combination the delicate spray stenciling technique, a stamped corrugated cardboard line, and a rollered stripe achieve an interesting contrast and make a lively design.

Brush-, Roller-, Reverse-stenciled, and Stamped Wall

This wall was rollered in white and beige, then stenciled using a roller in the same colors. The wreath was done using the wiped brush technique in cool beige. Inside the oval panel a reverse stencil of a tree was done over deep blue. The main area of the wall below the chair rail was stamped randomly, using corrugated paper and cool beige to break up the rigidity of the rest.

Making Cylinder Stamps with Rollers (see pp. 82–87)

Using Rollers (see pp. 44–47)

Using Stencil Brushes (see pp. 38–43)

Using Found Objects (see pp. 72–75)

Reverse Stenciling (see pp. 58–63)

Stamped and Brush-stenciled Box

RIGHT A border stencil design was applied in blue using brushes, on this red box. Pink, yellow, and orange dots were stamped around the design using nail heads.

Using Stencil Brushes (see pp. 38–43)

Using Found Objects (see pp. 72–75)

Rollered, Stamped and Brush-stenciled Box

BELOW AND RIGHT A small roller was used to make the stripes on the outside of this box, and thinner lines stamped with the edge of some corrugated cardboard to complete the tartan effect. On the inside, a small stencil design was applied with brushes.

Making Cylinder Stamps with Rollers (see pp. 82–87)

Using Found Objects (see pp. 72–75)

Using Stencil Brushes (see pp. 38–43)

Stamped, Brush-stenciled, and Reverse-stenciled Box

BELOW AND RIGHT A red box was covered randomly with circular stickers, and blue paint was applied both inside and out. Two shades of green paint were applied with small rollers. When the stickers were removed the original base color was apparent. The stencil inside the box was printed with brushes twice, with the design set off-register the second time.

Using Stencil Brushes (see pp. 38–43)

Reverse Stenciling (see pp. 58–63)

Making Cylinder Stamps with Rollers (see pp. 82–87)

Stamped and Brush-stenciled Fireplace

LEFT *This fireplace was painted dark blue, then stamped using a square of Styrofoam/polystyrene covered with a cool beige paint. A stencil design was then applied using brushes. Circles of yellow and blue paint were also stamped on it, using the rim of a lid.*

Designing Stamps
(see pp. 68–71)

Using Found Objects
(see pp. 72–75)

Using Stencil Brushes
(see pp. 38–43)

Stamped and Brush-stenciled Chest

BELOW AND RIGHT *A pale blue chest was frottaged in olive-green (see p. 13). It was then stamped with a novelty sponge in the shape of a whale. Lines like waves were also stamped, using the edge of some corrugated cardboard, and motifs were brush-stenciled around the edge.*

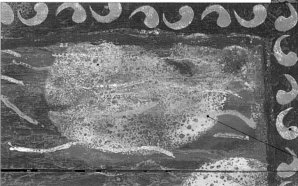

Using Stencil Brushes (see pp. 38–43)

Using Found Objects (see pp. 72–75)

*Using Spray
Paints (see
pp. 48–53)*

*Using Found
Objects (see
pp. 72–75)*

*Using Stencil Brushes
(see pp. 38–43)*

Sprayed, Brush-stenciled, and Stamped Table

*ABOVE RIGHT This small oval
table was painted dark
blue, then spray-stenciled
in white and yellow on
the top. Half of a cup rim
was used to stamp the
semicircles around the
edge. The legs were
brush-stenciled with
gold metallic wax.*

Rollered and Roller-stenciled Carpet

*BELOW Rollers were used on this piece of
heavy-duty canvas to create the uneven
effect in the border and the checked
pattern in the center. Four stencils
were applied using rollers.*

*Making Cylinder
Stamps with Rollers
(see pp. 82–87)*

*Using Rollers
(see pp. 44–47)*

Stamped and Brush-stenciled Wall

*LEFT Using potato halves,
blue spots in a loose
squared pattern were
stamped over this deep
brown wall. In between,
stencils of a flower, a dog,
a house, and a bird were
added in bright colors.*

*Making Stamps
(see pp. 76–81)*

*Using Stencil Brushes
(see pp. 38–43)*

Index

Suppliers

The following suppliers are listed in alphabetical order by county. For more information on Annie Sloan and Annie Sloan's Traditional Paints you can visit her Internet site on www.anniesloan.co.uk

ENGLAND

Home Makers
Bishop Centre Shopping
Village, Bath Road
Taplow, Berks, SL6 0NX

Jeremy Hancock
Fanny's
1 Lynmouth Road
Reading, Berks, RG1 8DD

Paint Effects at Windsor Fireplaces
339 St. Leonards Road
Windsor, Berks, SL4 3DS

The Natural Fabric Co.
Wessex Place
127 High Street
Hungerford, Berks
RG17 0DL

Painted Furniture
Unit 6 Clarence Mill
Bollington, Macclesfield
Cheshire, SK10 5JT

Wrights of Lymm Ltd
Millers Lane, Lymm
Cheshire, WA13 9RG

Cynthia Greenslade
The Granary, Treviskey
Portloe, Truro
Cornwall, TR2 5PN

Rooks Wood Workshop
The Old Vicarage
St. Clether
Nr Launceston
Cornwall, PL15 8UQ

Decorative Arts
5 Market Place
Melbourne
Derbys, DE73 1DS

The Stencil Shop
Eyam Hall Craft Centre
Eyam, Derbys, S30 1QW

Bailey Paints
Griffin Mill Est.
London Road
Thrupp, Nr Stroud
Glos, GL5 7AZ

Country Colours
20 West Way, Cirencester
Glos, GL7 1PY

Burwoods
60 The High Street
Lymington, Hants
SO41 9AH

Burwoods
14 The Square
Winchester, Hants
SO23 9ES

Neil Chambers
Trend of Worcester
14 Friar Street, Worcester
Hereford and Worcs
WR1 2RZ

Crafty Ideas
6 The Arcade, Hitchin
Herts, SG5 1ED

District Modern Stores
2 Vaughan Road
Harpenden
Herts, AL5 4ED

Artlines and Outlines
58 Glebe Way
West Wickham, Kent
BR4 0RL

Chromos
59 High Street
Tunbridge Wells, Kent
TN1 1XF

Half a Sixpence
Evegate Craft Centre
Station Road, Evegate
Smeeth, Ashford
Kent, TN25 6SX

Stencil Essentials at The Mad Hatters
26 High Street, Otford
Kent, TN14 5PQ

Harris Fine Art
712 High Road
North Finchley
London, N12 9QD

Vargail DIY and Paints
303–305 Cricklewood
Lane, London, NW2 2JL

M P Moran & Sons
297/301 Kilburn High
Road, London, NW6 7JS

S & S Home Supplies Ltd
16–18 Hale Lane
Mill Hill, London
NW7 3NX

Morse
264 Lee High Road
London, SE13 5PL

Mylands
80 Norwood High Street
London, SE27 9NW

Paint Service Co. Ltd
19 Eccleston Street
London, SW1W 9LX

Green and Stone
259 Kings Road
London, SW3 5EL

Michael Putman
151 Lavender Hill
London, SW11 5QJ

Lords Trade and DIY
119–121 Westbourne
Grove, London, W2 4UP

Interiors of Chiswick
454–458 Chiswick High
Road, London, W4 5TT

Askew Paint Centre
103 Askew Road
London, W12 9AS

Allpro Services
14–15 Station Parade
Northolt Road
South Harrow, Middx
HA2 8HB

Greenford Decor Centre Ltd
312–316 Ruislip Road East
Greenford, Middx
UB6 9BH

Paints 'n' Papers
394 Long Lane
Hillingdon
Middx, UB10 9PG

S & S Home Supplies Ltd
389–391 Honeypot Lane
Stanmore, Middx, HA7 1JJ

The Triumph Press
91 High Street, Edgware
Middx, HA8 7OB

Screens & Courses
Cherry House, High Street
Whixley, N. Yorks
YO5 8AW

Paint & Paper Ltd
11 Hellesdon Park Ind. Est.
Drayton Road, Norwich
Norfolk, NR6 5QR

E Milner Ltd
13 Lombard Street
Abingdon, Oxon
OX14 5BJ

E Milner (Oxford) Ltd
Canterbury Works,
Glanville Road, Oxford
OX4 2DB

Park End Antiques and Interiors
10 Park End Street
Oxford, OX1 1HH

Relics of Witney
(UK Distributor. Mail order
for Annie Sloan Traditional
Paint and Stencils)
35 Bridge Street, Witney
Oxon, OX8 6DA

Period House Shop
141 Corve Street, Ludlow
Shrops, SY8 2PG

Period House Shop
65 Wyle Cop, Shrewsbury
Shrops, SY1 1UX

Half a Sixpence
The Borough Mall
Wedmore, Somerset
BS28 4EB

Bryant and Goodall
Shop 3 Holliday Wharf
164 Holliday Street
Birmingham
W. Midlands, B1 1TJ

Gough Brothers
71A High Street
Bognor Regis, W. Sussex
PO21 1RZ

Welcome Home
18A Warwick Street
Worthing, W. Sussex
BN11 3DJ

SCOTLAND

Artstore
94 Queen Street
Glasgow, G1 3AQ

Acknowledgments

The same terrific team of people has been responsible for this book as for the other books in the same series. The combo in the studio were, on the light box Yawning Steve Wooster, on camera Memory Man Geoffrey Dann, and player of many parts Gavin the Cuban. The backup track was provided by Liz Penny by way of refreshments and props. In the office thanks as usual to Colin Ziegler, Claire Waite and Mandy Greenfield for their care and consideration in the tricky balancing act between text and pictures.

Back at home and in the paint studio my husband David Manuel and my children Henry, Felix and Hugo have all been tremendously supportive and helpful of an, at times, very cantankerous author. Many thanks also to Wendy Rawlins and Emma Brooklyn for good humoured help in trying to keep me tidy.

All the pieces in this book were painted using Annie Sloan paint products, including stencils, available form the stockists listed or through Relics of Witney mail order (see the list of suppliers on the previous page).

For the fire surround on page 58 thanks to R G Willis (Wessex Products Ltd, Unit 16 Harris Road, Calne Business Centre, Calne, Wilts. SN11 9PT Tel: 01249 813338). Thanks also to Jane Warwick for help in obtaining the blanks to work on.

Thanks also to Lewis Ward of Whistler Brushes, whose specialist brushes feature frequently throughout the book (Lewis Ward and Co., 128 Fortune Green Road, London, NW6 1DN Tel: 0171 794 3130), and all those at Relics of Witney, especially Bret Wiles, Chris Walker and Ray Russell for help with materials and advice.